531.14

Let's Investigate Science

Force & Motion

Force & Motion

Robin Kerrod

Illustrated by Ted Evans

Heinemann

First published in Great Britain by Heinemann Library
an imprint of Heinemann Publishers (Oxford) Ltd
Halley Court, Jordan Hill, Oxford OX2 8EJ

MADRID ATHENS PARIS
FLORENCE PRAGUE WARSAW
PORTSMOUTH NH CHICAGO SAO PAULO
SINGAPORE TOKYO MELBOURNE AUKLAND
IBADAN GABORONE JOHANNESBURG

Series created by Graham Beehag Book Design

99 98 97 96 95
10 9 8 7 6 5 4 3 2 1

Printed and bound in Hong Kong

British Library Cataloguing in Publication Data

Kerrod, Robin
Force and Motion. - (Let's Investigate Science Series)
I. Title II. Series
531.11

ISBN 0-431-07846-7

Contents

Introduction

Forces of one kind or another rule our everyday lives, our world and indeed the whole Universe. But what exactly are forces? Well, they can take many forms. They can be something obvious, like pushes and pulls, and hits and kicks.

Forces can also be invisible influences that we are barely aware of. One example is gravity, the pull the Earth exerts on everything in our world. Another is air pressure, a force that presses down on every square inch of our bodies.

All these forces that affect us are quite different, but they do have one thing in common. They almost always bring about, or try to bring about, movement. For example, a kick applied to a ball sets it in motion. Gravity tugs at leaves blown from a tree and makes them move downwards.

In this book we investigate the principles behind forces and the motions they create. We also see how various forces affect us and how we can often make use of them.

You can check your answers to the questions featured throughout this book on pages 59-62.

◄ A motorbike cornering at high speeds. As the rider leans over, gravity tugs at his body and threatens to pull him off. But because he is moving fast, other forces are set up that oppose gravity and keep him in his seat.

1 The Nature of Forces

9

◄ Horse and rider part company when the horse refuses a jump. The cantering horse suddenly stops, but the rider, because of his inertia, keeps going.

When horses stop and riders don't, and balloons whiz crazily through the air, forces are at work. This chapter looks at the nature of forces and begins with basic laws that relate to forces and the motion they set up.

In the 1630s, the Italian scientist Galileo was one of the first to investigate experimentally the relationships between force and motion. But it was the English genius Isaac Newton who first stated these relationships in detail, as his three laws of motion.

Newton's laws were published in 1687 in what is perhaps the most important science book ever printed, *Philosophiae Naturalis Principia Mathematica*, usually known as the *Principia*. This work also included Newton's theory of gravity, a revolutionary new form of mathematics called calculus, and a wealth of other pioneering work in many branches of science.

▼ When you blow up a balloon and let it go, it whooshes away, propelled by jet propulsion. The force of the air shooting out backwards sets up an equal and opposite force that propels the balloon forwards.

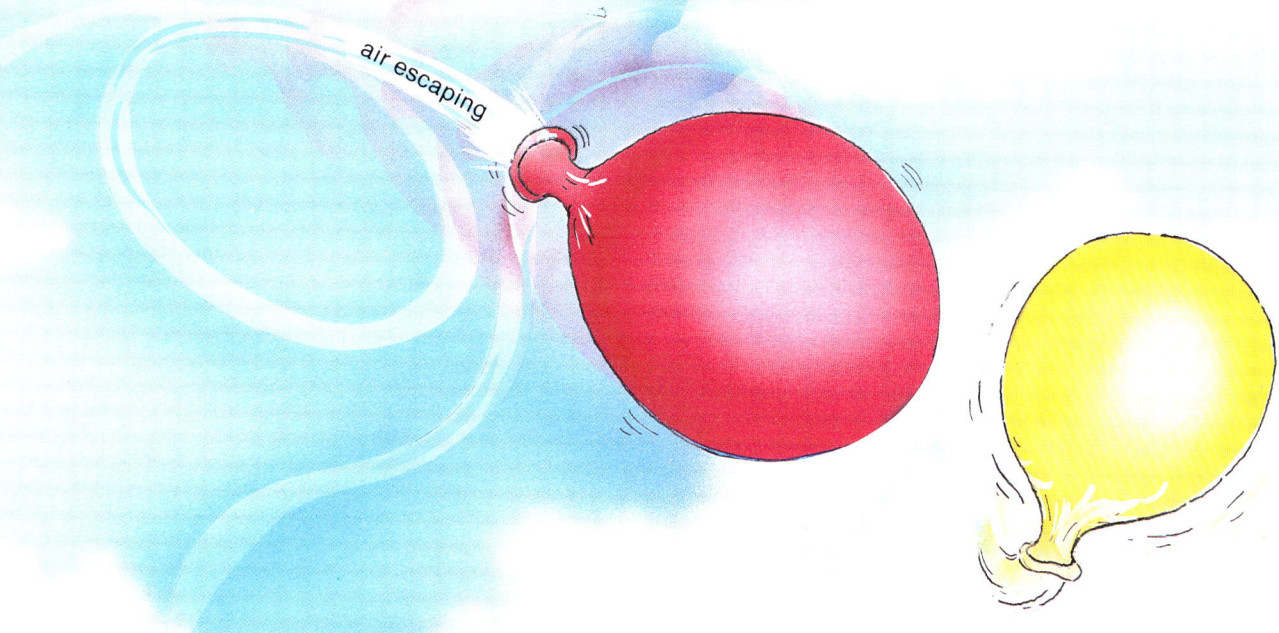

air escaping

Laws of motion

When no one is playing, the balls on a pool table don't move. They are at rest. Each ball will remain at rest until you hit it, that is, apply a force to it. The same is true for any body at rest: it remains at rest until it is acted upon by a force.

When you throw a cricket ball, it will keep on moving straight until someone hits it or catches it; that is, until a force of some kind acts on it either to change its direction or to stop it.

10

Isaac Newton summed up these observations as his first law of motion: each body continues in a state of rest or in uniform motion in a straight line unless it is acted upon by a force. ('Uniform' here means 'at the same speed'.)

Newton's second law of motion describes what happens to a body when it is acted on by a force. The force causes the body to change speed. The rate at which the body's speed changes, that is, its acceleration (a), depends on the size of the force (F). It also depends on the mass (m) of the body. Mathematically, we can express this in the equation: $F = ma$.

▼ **This 'executive toy' is known as Newton's cradle. When you let the end ball on one side swing down to hit the others, the end ball on the other side swings up. The middle balls, which can't easily move, transmit forces to the end ones, which are able to move.**

? 1. What do you think would happen if you let two balls swing down?

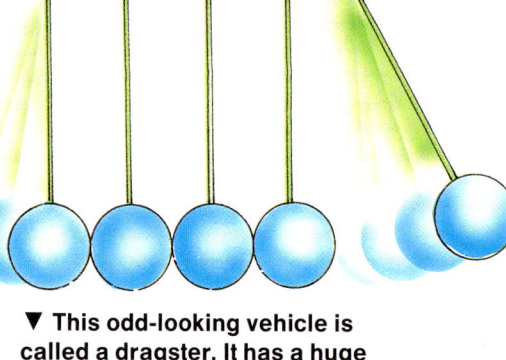

▼ **This odd-looking vehicle is called a dragster. It has a huge engine to give it the fastest possible acceleration. Dragsters race each other over a track 402 metres long.**

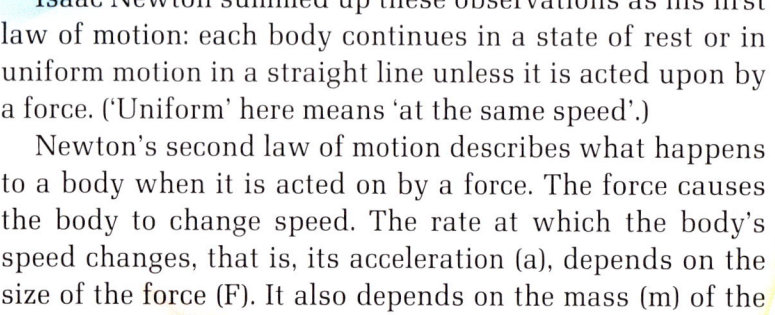

▲ **A Titan-Centaur rocket blasts off the launch pad at Cape Canaveral, Florida, USA, with a thrust of 1,200,000 kg. Reaction to the hot gases shooting backwards out of the rocket nozzles gives rise to the forward thrust that propels the rocket.**

Newton's third law

The third law of motion stated by Newton says that to every action there is an equal and opposite reaction. In other words, when a force acts on a body, that body also exerts back an equal force. When you push against a wall, the wall pushes back at you.

The third law, also called the reaction principle, explains how rockets work.

11

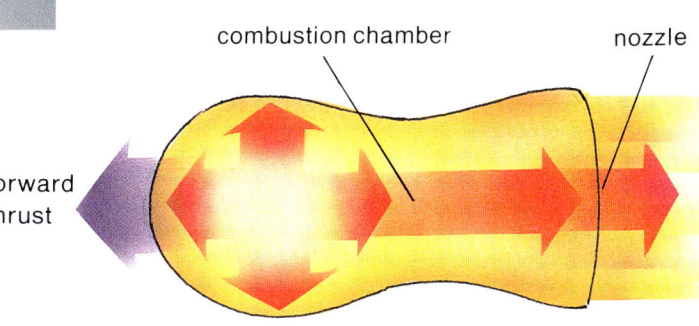

combustion chamber   nozzle

forward thrust

In a rocket, fuel is introduced into a combustion chamber and burned. The hot gases produced shoot out of the engine nozzle at high speed. By Newton's third law, the 'action' of the gases shooting out of the nozzle is accompanied by an equal and opposite 'reaction', that is, by an equal force acting in the opposite direction. This is the force, called thrust, that drives the rocket forward.

INVESTIGATE

Take an empty plastic bottle and find a cork to fit the mouth. Lay out half-a-dozen round pencils on a flat surface. Put a few teaspoonfuls of baking soda (sodium bicarbonate) into the bottle, then pour in a little vinegar. Quickly push in the cork, but not too tightly. Now place the bottle on its side on the pencils.

? What happens to the bottle when the cork pops out?

12

Tricky!

◀ Build a pile of draughts. How can you take out the one at the bottom without knocking down the others?

▼ You have two identical eggs. One is uncooked, the other is hard-boiled. How can you tell them apart without breaking them?

▶ Car makers test new designs by crashing them against a wall. The wall stops the front part of the car, but, because of inertia, the rest of the car continues moving, causing the body to crumple. Designers must insure that in a crash the passenger compartment remains as rigid as possible.

Resisting change

As we saw earlier (see page 10), a body that is still tends to stay still, and a body that is moving tends to keep on moving. We call this tendency of a body to remain in its existing state its inertia. Inertia is one of the basic properties of matter.

Inertia affects us in many ways. If you pull a full glass of water towards you suddenly, the water slops over the opposite side as it tries to stay where it is. When you stop moving the glass, the water now slops over the near side of the glass as it tries to keep on moving.

If you are travelling fast on your bike and suddenly jam on the brakes, your body is thrown forward. It tries to keep moving as before.

Using inertia, we can also do tricks (see left).

Momentum

A measure of a body's resistance to a change in motion is given by its momentum. Momentum equals mass times velocity (speed in a certain direction). Because of its extra mass, a heavy lorry has a larger momentum than a family car travelling at the same speed. The heavy lorry has more momentum at high speed than it does at low speed.

► When a golfer drives off the tee or makes a putt, the ball experiences resisting forces that make it slow down.

? 1. What is the main resisting force the ball experiences (A) in a drive, (B) in a putt?

IT'S AMAZING!

We can get perpetual motion of a sort in superconductors. These are metals that are cooled to very low temperatures (as low as $-270°C$). Once you set an electric current flowing in a superconductor, it just keeps on flowing. The electrical resistance of the metal vanishes.

Friction

Another force is involved whenever movement takes place. This is friction. It is a resisting force set up between the surface of the moving body and its surroundings. An aircraft experiences friction with the air it flies through, which we call air resistance or drag (see page 38). The moving parts of machines experience friction, which is reduced by keeping them well oiled.

Vehicles and machines consume a lot of power in overcoming friction. But friction is useful too. Without it, we couldn't walk, we couldn't nail things together, and we would have no brakes for our cars.

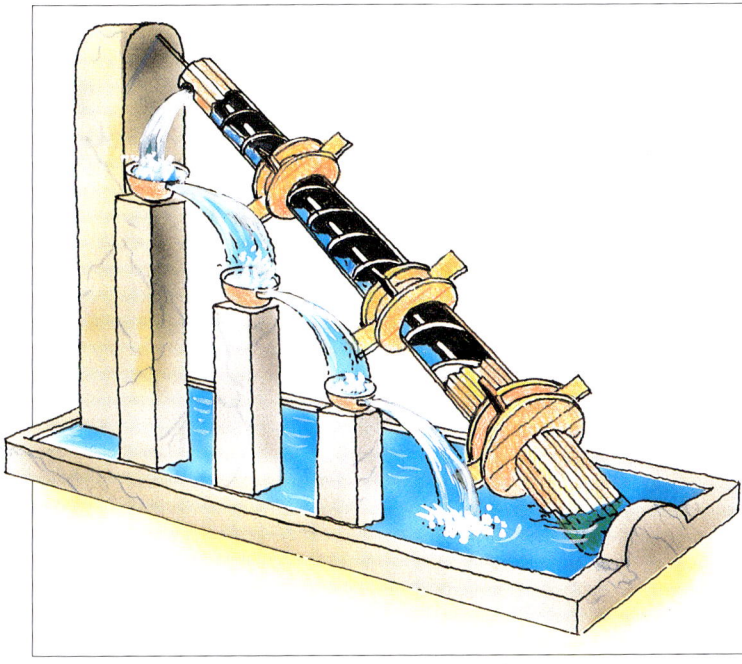

Motion without end

For centuries inventors tried to build machines which, once working, would keep on going by themselves. They would produce perpetual motion. The diagram shows one idea for a perpetual-motion machine. It consists of a water-lifting device called an Archimedean screw, on which are mounted a number of waterwheels. As the water falls down, it spins the waterwheels, making the screw rotate. The rotating screw then carries the water up again.

? 2. Perpetual-motion machines can't be built. Why?

Speed and direction

You are riding your bike along the road at a speed of 16 km/h (10 mph). What does this tell us? It tells us how far you will go in a certain time, but it doesn't tell us where you will get to. This depends on the direction in which you are travelling.

To specify your journey more precisely, therefore, we must know both your speed *and* the direction you take. We call speed in a certain direction the velocity. If you pedal at 16 km/h (10 mph) in a southerly direction, your velocity will be 16 km/h (10 mph) south.

Velocity is a quantity we call a vector, which has direction as well as size. Force and acceleration are vectors, too. For example, to describe what happens when something is hit by a force, we must know in which direction the force acts.

14

▲ Sailing boats cannot only sail with the wind, they can also sail into the wind. They do this by zig-zagging to the left and right of the direction in which the wind is blowing. This technique is called tacking.

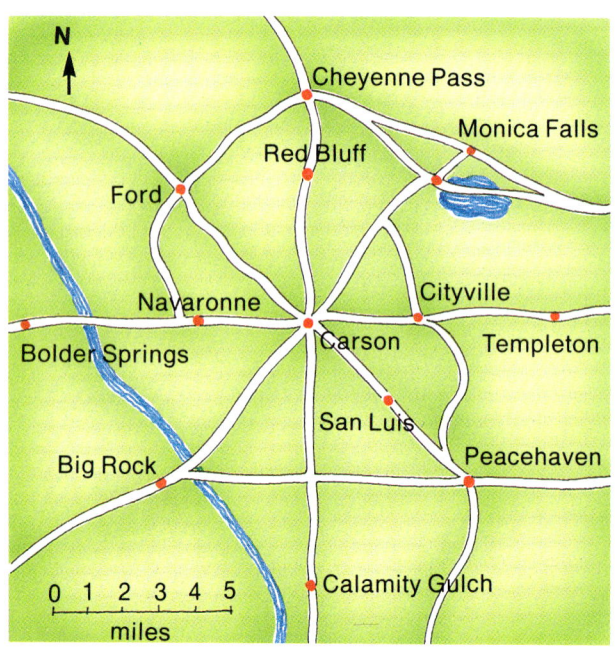

WORKOUT

Imagine you have just been given a new bike for your birthday and want to show it off to your friends, who live in neighbouring towns around your home of Cityville.

However, there are a few problems. All the signposts in the area have been removed for repainting. You have lost your map and your friends have to give you directions from the maps they have.

You live 6 miles due west of George. To reach Emma, you travel 3 miles west and then turn due south for 7 miles. Bill says he lives 13 miles north of Emma. Dawn says she lives 11 miles southwest of Karen.

Using the map (left) work out in which towns do these friends live? How long will it take you to reach them if you travel at a speed of 10 mph?

WORKOUT

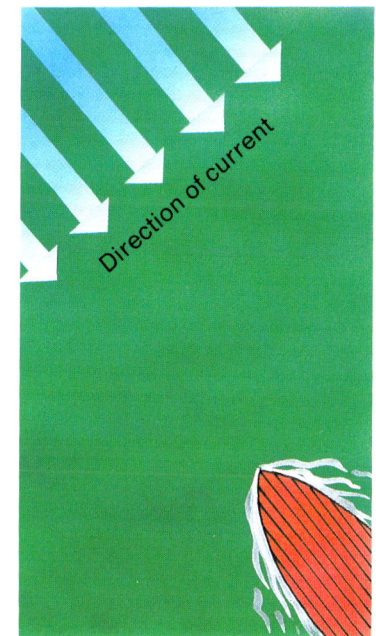

Direction of current

A boat is travelling across the sea, but it's progress is being affected by the current. It is moving through the water at a speed of 30 km/h (19 mph) in a northeasterly direction. The current, however, is carrying the water in a southwesterly direction at 11 km/h (7 mph).

What is the resulting velocity (speed *and* direction) of the boat? What would be its resulting velocity if the current was flowing in a northeasterly direction?

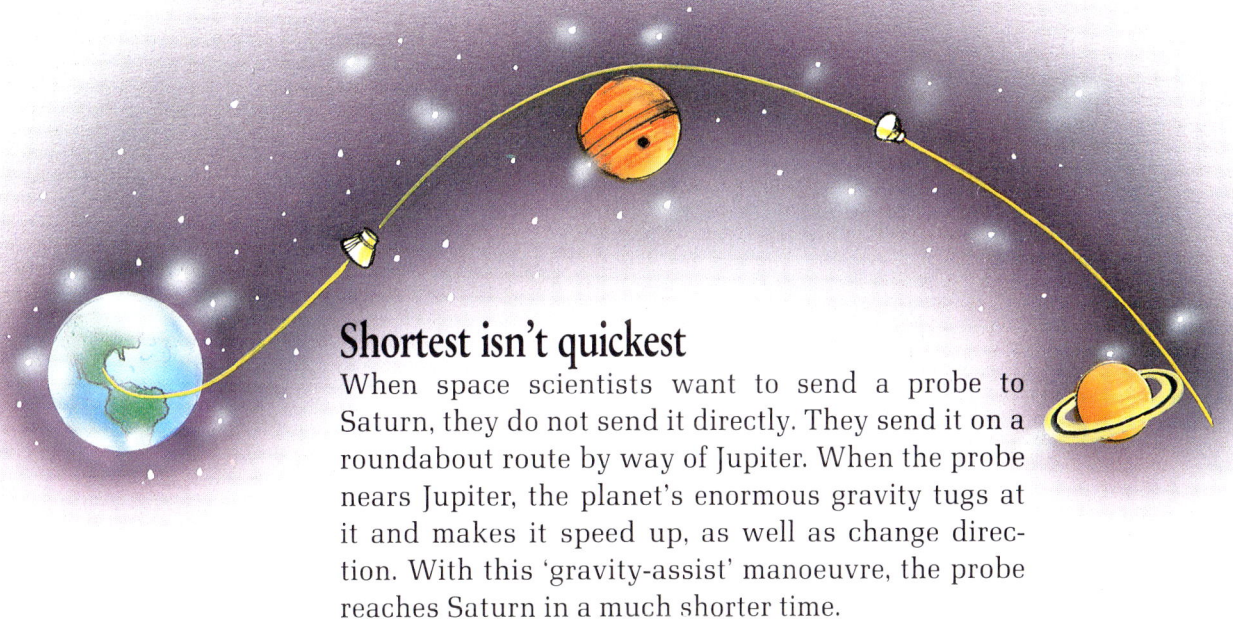

Shortest isn't quickest

When space scientists want to send a probe to Saturn, they do not send it directly. They send it on a roundabout route by way of Jupiter. When the probe nears Jupiter, the planet's enormous gravity tugs at it and makes it speed up, as well as change direction. With this 'gravity-assist' manoeuvre, the probe reaches Saturn in a much shorter time.

Turning forces

When we unscrew the lid of a jar, turn a door knob or undo a nut with a wrench, we exert a turning force. Let's consider the wrench and the nut. We can increase the turning effect we exert on the nut in two ways. We can increase the force we apply to the handle of the wrench. We can also increase the length of the handle, which gives us more leverage.

The turning effect about a point equals the force applied (**F**) multiplied by the perpendicular distance (**d**) between it and the point.

Or, turning effect $= \mathbf{F} \times \mathbf{d}$.

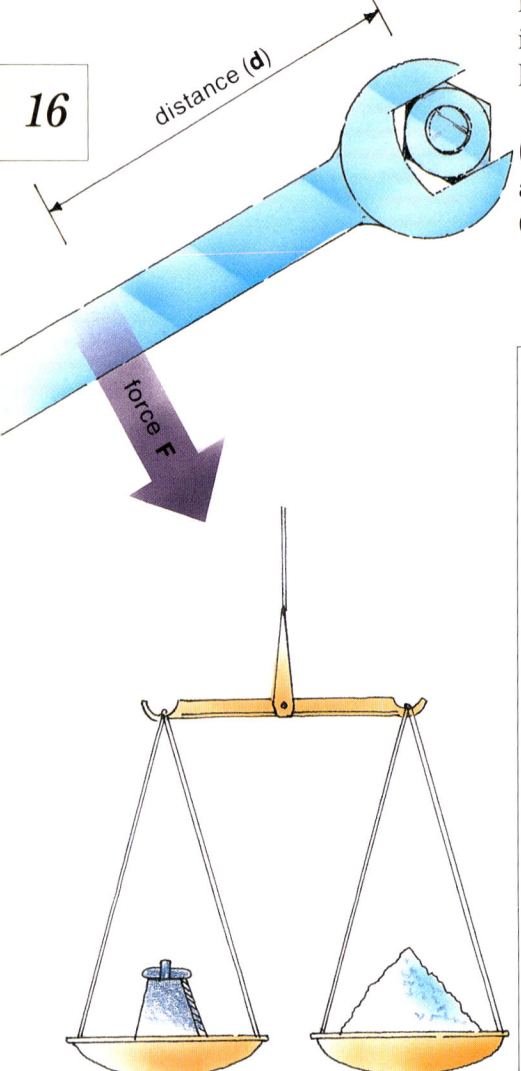

16

distance (**d**)

force **F**

▲ Simple hand scales use the balancing of turning effects to weigh things. Weights are added to one dish, and the material to be weighed is added to the other. When the arm is horizontal, the dishes are the same weight and balance each other.

INVESTIGATE

You can study turning effects using a ruler and some coins. Balance the ruler on a pencil, then place a coin on one side. It tips up, of course. So place a similar coin on the other side until the ruler is balanced again. Note the distance between the centre of each coin and the fulcrum, or point of balance. What do you notice?

Now put two coins on one side, and balance them with a single coin on the other. Measure the distances between the coins and the fulcrum. Repeat the investigation using different numbers of coins on each side to make the ruler balance.

Work out the turning effects on each side of the fulcrum, taking the weight of one coin as a unit of force. (For example, the turning effect of two coins, 5 cm from the fulcrum would be 2×5.)

◄ Chinese circus acrobats perform a gravity-defying balancing feat with a bicycle. They do not topple over, because all the turning forces acting in the bicycle-and-bodies system are in balance.

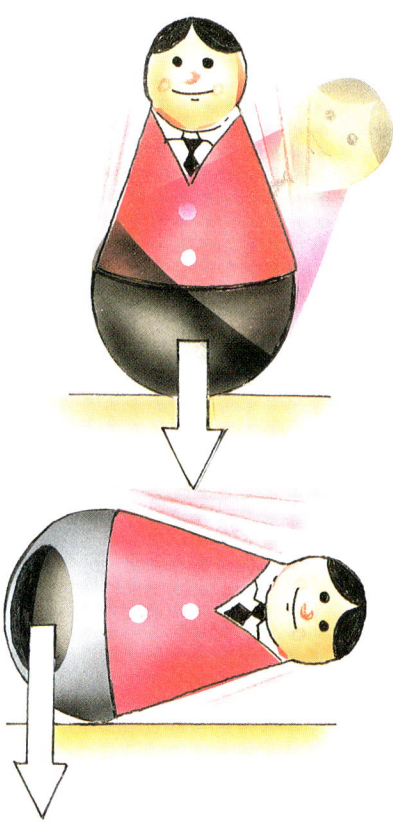

▲ This toy always returns to an upright position, even when knocked on its side.

❓ Can you see how it works?

In balance

From the INVESTIGATION, you should find that when the ruler is balanced, the turning effect of the coins on one side of the fulcrum is equal to the turning effect of the coins on the other side.

When the ruler is balanced, we say that it is in equilibrium. In other words, in equilibrium, all the turning forces acting on a body are in balance.

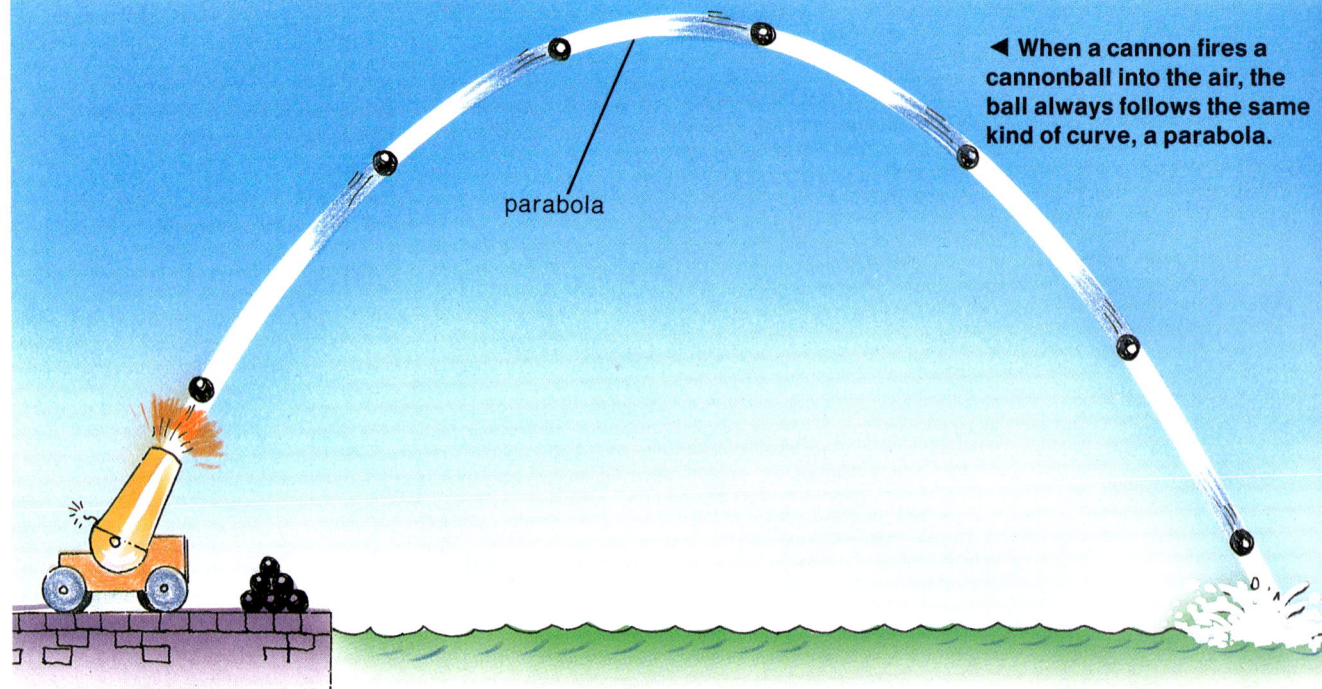

parabola

◄ When a cannon fires a cannonball into the air, the ball always follows the same kind of curve, a parabola.

Moving in curves and circles

When a cannonball is fired from a cannon, it follows a curved path, or trajectory. At any point in its path, the ball is trying to shoot off in a straight line. But the pull of gravity creates a resultant force that sends the ball into a curving path. The ball follows the curve of a parabola. Anything thrown into the air follows a similar path.

The study of the paths of bodies travelling through the air is called ballistics. It is important in the design of rockets and missiles, guns and artillery.

Circular motion

If you tie a ball to a piece of string and whirl it round your head, it travels in a circular path, of course. Notice that the string tugs at your hand. To keep the ball moving in a circle, you have to tug back. If you let go of the string, the ball shoots off in a straight line.

We call the tugging force that must be exerted on a body to make it travel in a circle the centripetal force. The word 'centripetal' means 'towards the centre'.

A satellite keeps circling the Earth because a centripetal force acts upon it. This force is the force of gravity. (See page 53.)

▲ When the water in a fountain shoots up into the air, it curves over in the shape of a parabola. When water spurts from many jets in a fountain, the falling water takes on a three-dimensional shape called a paraboloid.

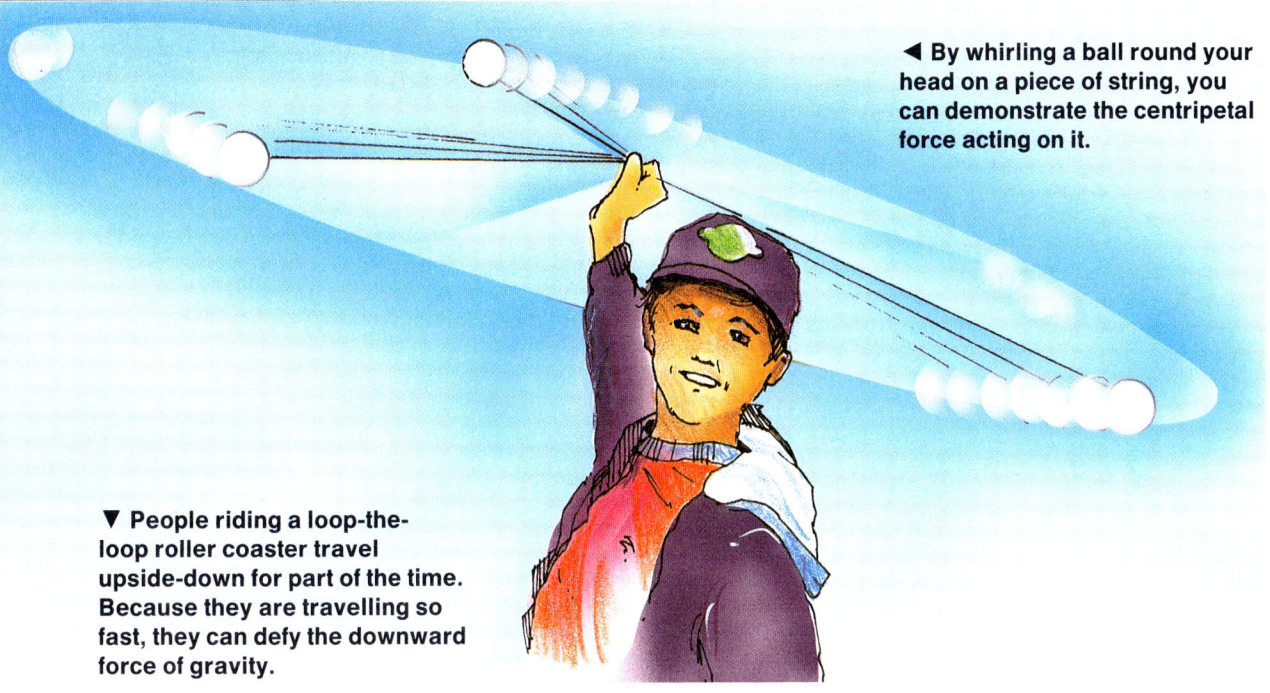

◀ **By whirling a ball round your head on a piece of string, you can demonstrate the centripetal force acting on it.**

▼ **People riding a loop-the-loop roller coaster travel upside-down for part of the time. Because they are travelling so fast, they can defy the downward force of gravity.**

▼ **Because of their rapidly spinning wheels, gyroscopes can perform amazing balancing acts. They can perch on the point of a pencil and balance on a thread.**

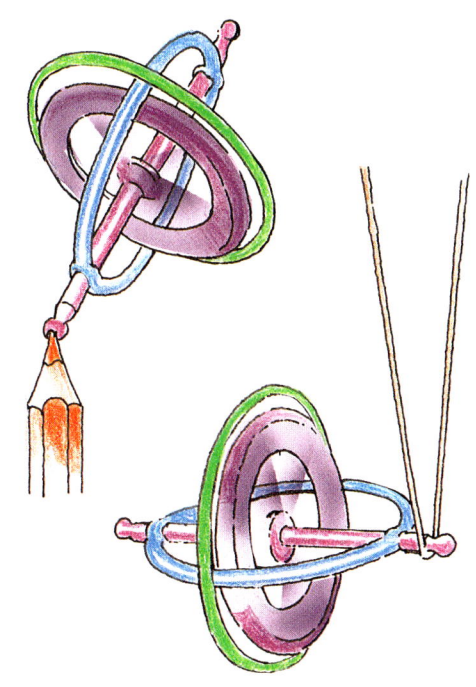

Spinning bodies

Bodies that spin have some interesting properties. Like all moving bodies, they have momentum (see page 12), which is a measure of their resistance to a change in motion. In the case of spinning bodies, it is called angular momentum.

It is the angular momentum of their spinning wheels that gives gyroscopes their surprising properties. It is also because of angular momentum that skaters can spin faster when they draw in their arms.

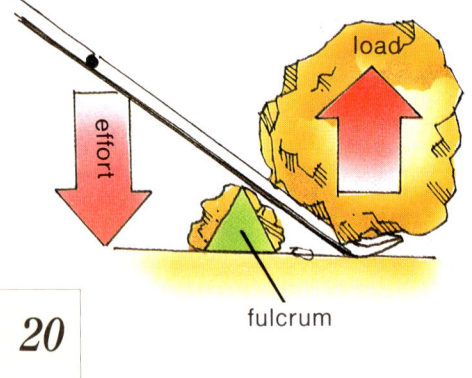

fulcrum

20

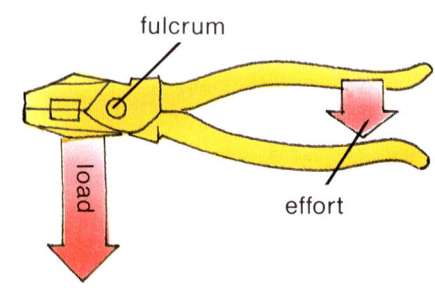

fulcrum

effort

Simple machines

A machine is a device that performs work. More simply, it is a device that applies a force (effort) at one point to overcome a force (load) at another.

Many of our machines are incredibly complicated. For example, a typical family car is made up of as many as 15,000 different components, from tiny nuts and bolts to the engine block and body panels. The main moving parts are there to carry the motion of the engine pistons to the driving wheels.

There are, however, some very simple machines, which hardly seem like machines at all. They include the lever, the inclined plane and the screw.

A crowbar is an example of a lever. You can 'lever up' a heavy box (load) with a crowbar by resting it on a low block of wood (fulcrum) and pressing down (effort) on the handle. By applying a small effort over a large distance, you can raise a large load a small distance.

The ratio of load to effort in a machine is called the mechanical advantage. It is a measure of how effective the machine is.

The inclined plane

This simple 'machine' is little more than a slope! An example is a plank placed from the ground into the back of a

The story of the wheel
Before the wheel came into use, people hauled heavy loads on log rollers. Without knowing it, they had found that rolling friction is less than sliding friction.

The first wheels were made from slices cut off logs. These were split in two, and then a semicircular hole was made in each part to fit an axle.

The Ancient Egyptians used spoked wheels for their fast war chariots. The wheel rim was made of wood and was shaped by being heated in a fire.

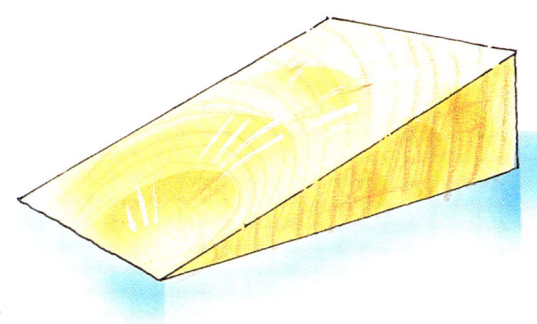

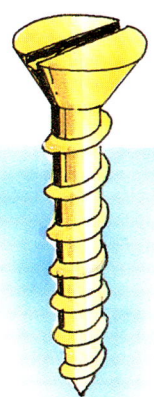

builder's truck. It is easier to push a wheelbarrow of sand up this plank than it is to lift the wheelbarrow vertically into the truck.

A wedge is a kind of inclined plane; so is a screw. With a screw, the inclined plane is cut at an angle round the screw body. When you rotate the screw once, it only advances the width of one thread.

Other simple machines are the wheel and axle (see Glossary, page 58) and the pulley, which is a variation of it.

The invaluable wheel

The wheel isn't really a machine. But in one guise or another, it forms an essential part of most machines. It appeared in the Middle East before 3200 BC.

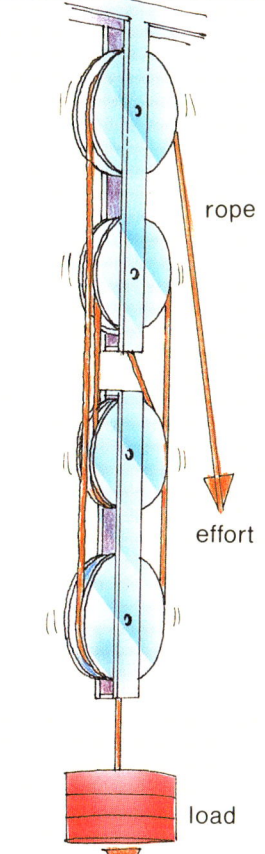

rope

effort

load

Pulleys

A pulley block has a number of grooved wheels, which can rotate on axles. It is suspended from a beam, and a load is hung from the bottom. The load is lifted by pulling on a rope threaded through the wheels. In this pulley, pulling out 60 cm of rope lifts the load by 15 cm.

❓ What effort would be required to lift a load of 100 newtons (10 kg)?

In Roman times the wheel was modified into the waterwheel. Driven by flowing water, this provided the first reliable mechanical power source.

Today, the wheel is widely found, not only in wheel form, but also in the form of toothed gears. Gearwheels transmit motion and change gear speeds.

Relatively speaking

If you pedal hard when you are riding your bike, you should be able to reach a speed of 30 km/h (20 mph) or more. To be precise, you should reach that speed relative to the ground.

If you are riding alongside a friend travelling at the same speed, your speed relative to your friend is zero. But if your friend is riding towards you at the same speed, then your speed relative to your friend will be 60 km/h (40 mph).

In other words, speed is a relative quantity.

Let's take this argument to its logical conclusion and investigate a fly named Fred. Is he the fastest fly in the Universe?

▲ **This is Fred, an ordinary housefly, member of the species** *Musca domestica*.

One day by chance Fred buzzes into the cabin of a Concorde, standing on the runway at Heathrow airport. Before you can say 'sonic boom', the cabin door has closed, and Fred has become supersonic and is on his way to America.

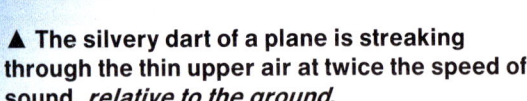

▲ **The silvery dart of a plane is streaking through the thin upper air at twice the speed of sound,** *relative to the ground*.

▼ **BUT: the ground is moving too, because the Earth spins on its axis in space once every 24 hours. It spins towards the east – in the same direction in which the Concorde is flying.**

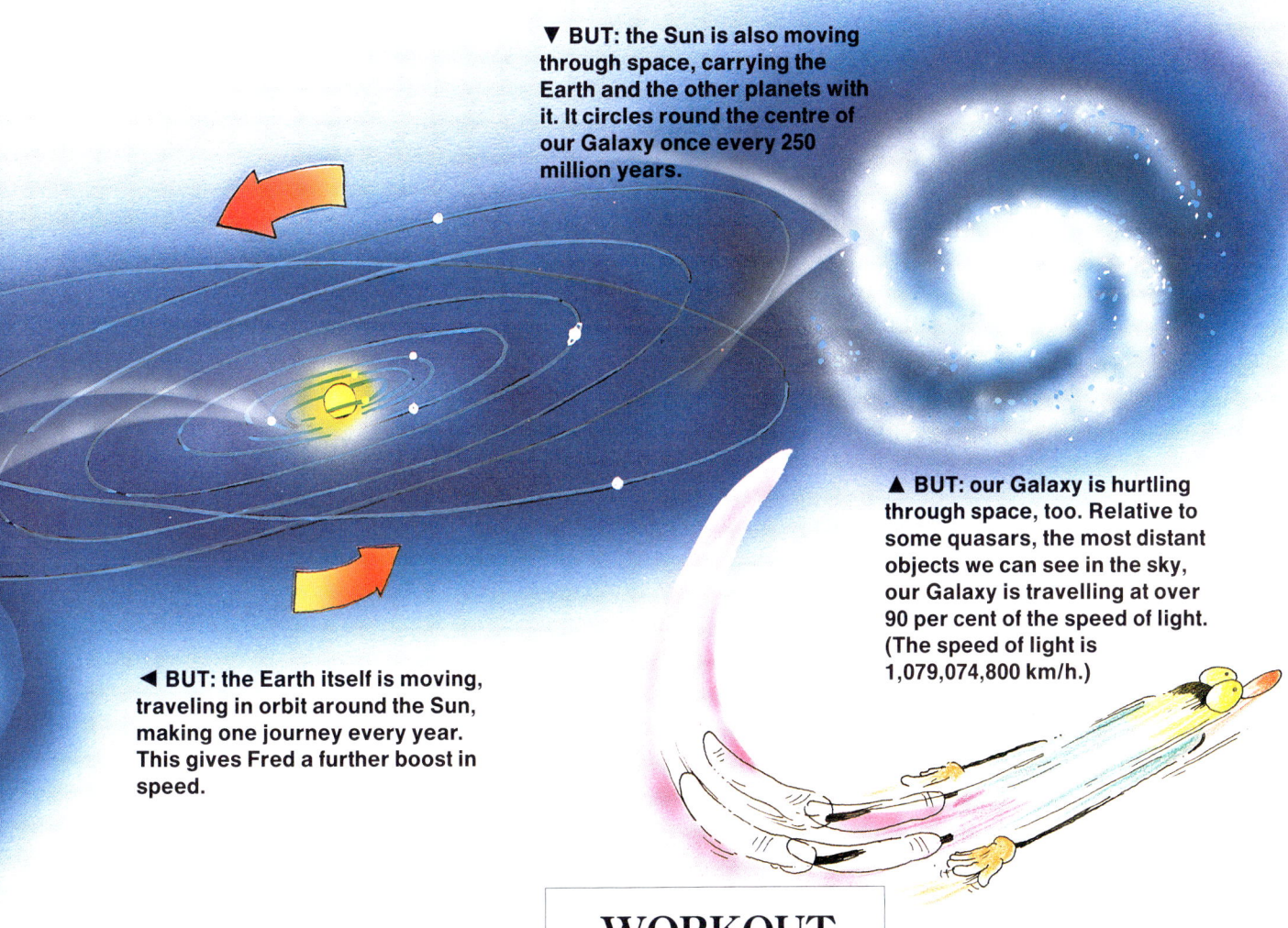

▼ BUT: the Sun is also moving through space, carrying the Earth and the other planets with it. It circles round the centre of our Galaxy once every 250 million years.

▲ BUT: our Galaxy is hurtling through space, too. Relative to some quasars, the most distant objects we can see in the sky, our Galaxy is travelling at over 90 per cent of the speed of light. (The speed of light is 1,079,074,800 km/h.)

◄ BUT: the Earth itself is moving, traveling in orbit around the Sun, making one journey every year. This gives Fred a further boost in speed.

WORKOUT

Using simple mathematics and the data given, figure out the following:

? 1. How fast Fred is moving relative to the ground.

? 2. How fast Fred is circling round the Earth's axis.

? 3. How fast Fred is circling in orbit round the Sun.

? 4. How fast Fred is circling in orbit round the Galaxy.

? 5. How fast Fred is moving, as seen from the most distant quasars.

The data you need:

Fred buzzes around happily in the Concorde's cabin at a speed of about 8 km/h (5 mph).

The speed of sound high in the atmosphere is about 1,100 km/h (684 mph).

The diameter of the Earth is 12,800 km.

The distance from the Earth to the Sun is 150,000,000 km.

The Sun lies 30,000 light-years away from the centre of the Galaxy.

1 light-year = 10,000,000,000,000 km (10^{13} km).

2
Forces All Around Us

◀ **A hot-air balloon rises into the air because of upthrust, a force acting on it because it is lighter than the surrounding air.**

▼ **Fish have their typical streamlined 'fish-shape' because it creates the least resistance, or drag, when they move through the water. Flying fish take advantage of aerodynamics to escape their pursuers.**

Forces are at work all the time in the world around us, and we must learn to understand them if we are to use them to our advantage.

For example, studying the forces in solid materials helps us design sky-scraping buildings and long, graceful bridges across rivers and estuaries. Studying the forces in liquids helps us design steel ships that float on the surface and submarines that travel under it. Studying the forces in gases helps us design aeroplanes that fly like birds.

Forces cannot only create motion, they can also oppose motion. In liquids and gases this forceful opposition takes the form of drag. Overcoming drag is one of the main concerns of aircraft and vehicle designers.

Forces between molecules

All the materials we come across in our everyday lives exist in one of three forms, or states. They are either solids, like rock; liquids, like water; or gases, like air.

All materials, whether solid, liquid or gas, are composed of billions of atoms (see page 42). Mostly, the atoms occur in groups as units called molecules. The physical properties of materials depend largely on the behaviour of their molecules and the forces they exert on one another.

(see page 42)

26

▼ The molecules behave differently in solids, liquids and gases, which gives these materials quite different properties.

solid   liquid   gas

IT'S AMAZING!

In 1 cm³ (cubic centimetre) of air at room temperature and pressure, there are about 27,000,000,000,000,000,000 (27 million million million or 2.7×10^{19}) molecules.

Kinetic theory

In a solid, the molecules are bound firmly to one another. In a liquid, the molecules can move around. In a gas, the molecules are far apart and move very fast; they hardly affect one another at all. This explanation of the nature of matter is called the kinetic theory.

Tension at the surface

One effect of the forces between molecules in a liquid is to give it a kind of 'skin'. This effect is called surface tension. It is the result of there being an overall downward force on the molecules at the surface of a liquid.

▲ This insect is called a pond skater or water strider, because it skates about on the surface of ponds.

? 2. Why doesn't it sink?

Pour a glass of water. What do you notice where the water meets the glass? The water curves up, forming what is called a meniscus. This happens because there is a force of attraction between glass and water molecules as well as between water molecules themselves.

? 1. What happens when you place a narrow glass tube in water?

INVESTIGATE

You wouldn't think that a sieve can hold water, would you? But it can. Prove this for yourself. You will need a flour sieve (make sure it's clean) and a bottle (or jar) with a neck up to about 5 cm across.

Fill the bottle right to the brim with water, and place the sieve firmly over it. Keeping the sieve in place, turn the bottle upside-down.

Although some of the water might run out to start with, most will stay in the bottle.

If you don't manage to do it right the first time, try again – it really does work! It works because the water in the small holes forms a 'skin' caused by surface tension.

? Another force is also involved. What is it?

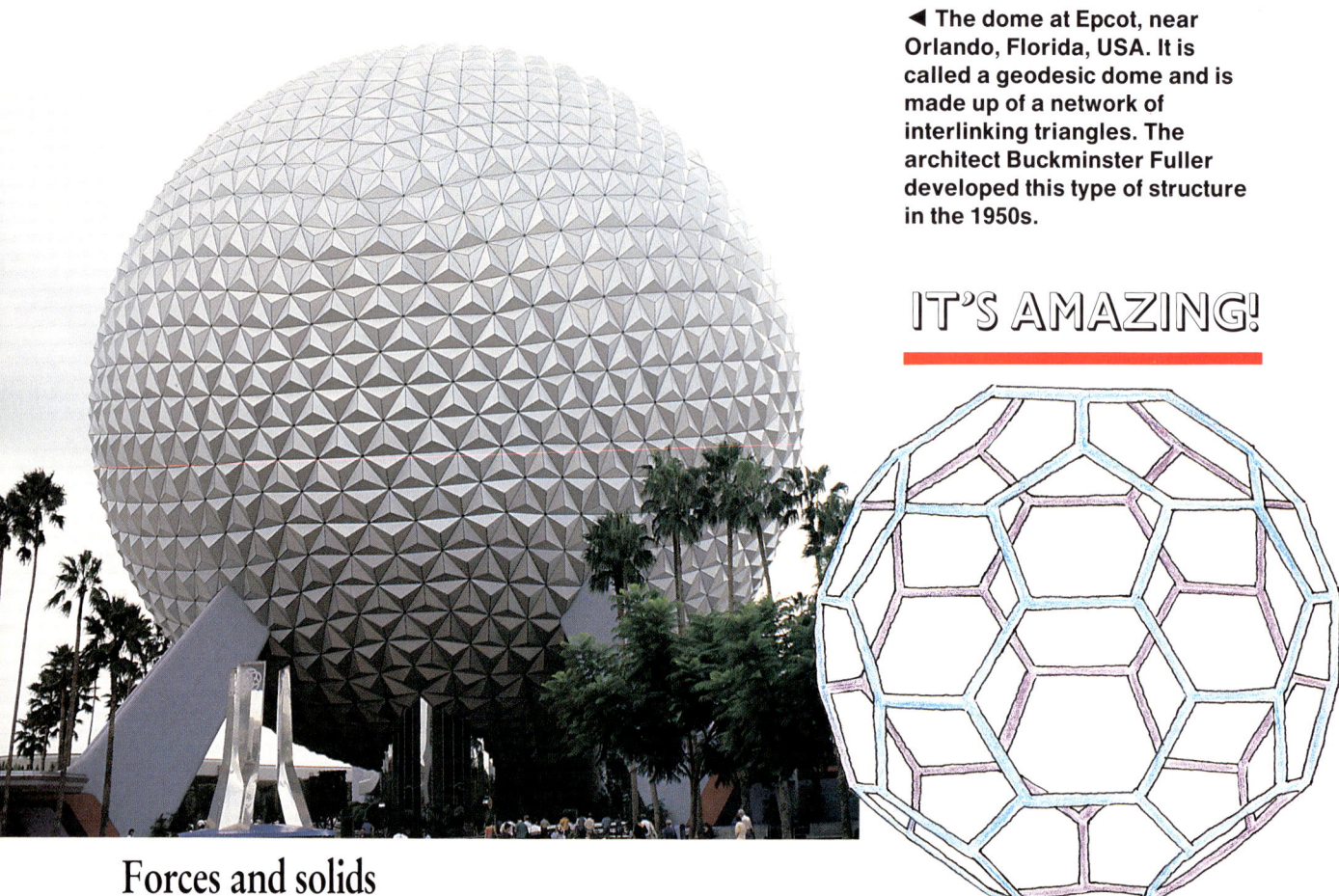

◄ The dome at Epcot, near Orlando, Florida, USA. It is called a geodesic dome and is made up of a network of interlinking triangles. The architect Buckminster Fuller developed this type of structure in the 1950s.

IT'S AMAZING!

This is a diagram of a molecule of a rare third form of natural carbon, only discovered in 1990. It looks like the dome structure invented by Buckminster Fuller. This form of carbon has therefore been called buckminsterfullerene. The dome-like molecule is nicknamed a 'buckyball'.

? **2.** What are the other two natural forms of carbon?

Forces and solids

In the modern world engineers have designed beautiful structures – buildings, bridges, aeroplanes, and so on. They must be concerned about the safety of their structures as well as the beauty. So they must insure that their designs can stand up to the forces they will have to bear in practice.

In particular, the designers must choose the right materials of construction, because different materials behave differently under the action of forces.

For example, concrete behaves differently to steel. You can build a fairly long bridge using a steel beam. But you can't build one using a long slab of concrete. The concrete sags in the middle and breaks. This is because it's weak when it is pulled or under tension. Steel, however, is strong under tension. We say it has high tensile strength. Many metals are like this.

? **1.** What is the force that causes the concrete to sag?

Concrete construction

Concrete is widely used in construction, however, because it is cheap. But it is almost always reinforced, or strengthened. This is done by including in the concrete steel rods or cables. These give it tensile strength and keep it from sagging.

Concrete by itself can be used to build strong arch bridges. This is because in arch bridges materials are under squeezing, or compression, forces. Concrete is very strong under compression. We say it has high compressive strength.

Strong elastic

Steel structures also have another property that helps make them safe. They are able to 'give', or stretch, slightly when extra forces act on them. Afterwards, they return to their original size and shape. Skyscrapers like the Empire State Building in New York sway several inches or more when a gale blows, but remain perfectly safe.

Steel, then, is slightly elastic. But if too big a force is applied to it, it becomes permanently stretched, and it may even break.

▲ The famous Golden Gate Bridge, across the entrance to San Francisco Bay, USA. The bridge is built mainly of steel. The bridge deck is suspended from cables made up of thousands of strands of steel wire.

? What is this kind of bridge called?

▼ Roman engineers built this arch bridge in southern Spain about 1,800 years ago. They knew that stone, like concrete, is strong when compressed.

Pressure in liquids

In the INVESTIGATION (below), water spurts from the holes in the bottle with some speed. Clearly, some force is driving it. It is the force we call water pressure.

In science, the term 'pressure' has a precise meaning. It is the force acting per unit area, and it is measured in newtons per square metre called 'pascals' (Pa). Meteorologists (weather forecasters) use other units such as millibars (mb).

The pressure at a certain depth within a liquid is due to the weight of the column of liquid above it pressing down. This weight depends on the depth and also on the density of the liquid. Thus, pressure too depends on depth and density.

Pressure in the sea

Because it is deep, the sea can exert enormous pressure on bodies within it. For every 10 metres you go down, the pressure increases by 1 atmosphere. (One atmosphere is the normal pressure of the atmosphere at sea level, about 100,000 Pa.) To counter the pressure of the water, deep-sea divers have to work in suits supplied with compressed air.

▲ A road runs along the top of the Hoover Dam on the Arizona/Nevada border. Standing 221 metres high, it is the highest concrete dam in the United States. Completed in 1936, it is a favourite tourist attraction.

? 1. Which river does it dam and what is the name of the reservoir behind the dam?

? 2. At the top, the dam is only a road's width acoss. Yet at the bottom, it is over 108 metres thick. Why is this necessary?

INVESTIGATE

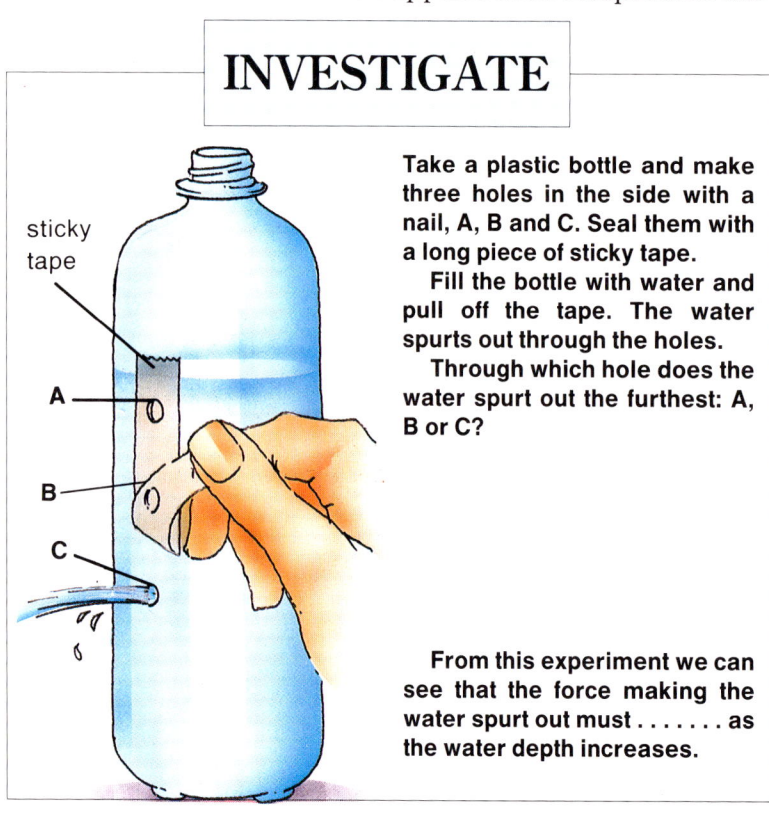

sticky tape

A

B

C

Take a plastic bottle and make three holes in the side with a nail, A, B and C. Seal them with a long piece of sticky tape.

Fill the bottle with water and pull off the tape. The water spurts out through the holes.

Through which hole does the water spurt out the furthest: A, B or C?

From this experiment we can see that the force making the water spurt out must . . . . as the water depth increases.

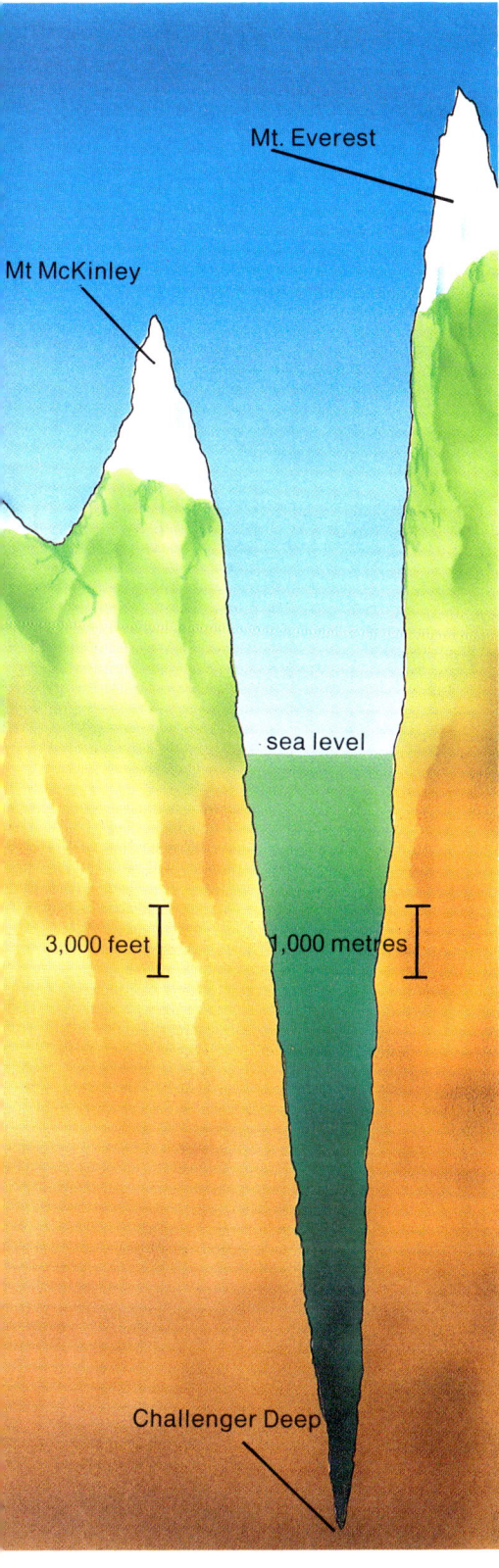

Mt. Everest

Mt McKinley

sea level

3,000 feet

1,000 metres

Challenger Deep

WORKOUT

The diagram left shows to scale the Pacific Ocean's Challenger Deep, compared with the heights of Mt. McKinley in Alaska and Mt. Everest in the Himalayas. By measurement, work out:

(A) How deep is Challenger Deep?

(B) How much is it deeper than Mt. McKinley and Mt. Everest are high?

(C) What is the pressure at the bottom of Challenger Deep? (Use the figures from the main text.)

▲ The U.S. Navy bathyscaphe *Trieste*, a deep-diving vessel that in January 1960 descended into Challenger Deep in the Pacific Ocean, about 400 km (250 miles) from the island of Guam. This is the deepest point in the oceans as far as we know.

Hydraulic pressure

You can't compress a liquid the same way as a gas (see page 34). If you apply a force to a liquid at one point, it travels throughout the liquid.

This principle of hydraulic pressure is used in many machines to transmit power. For example, car brakes work by hydraulic pressure, and so do the arms of steam shovels and the moving control surfaces of aircraft.

32

INVESTIGATE

Carry out this experiment to investigate the forces acting inside liquids. You will need a simple spring balance and a pair of scales like those you find in the kitchen; a heavy object like a stone; and a jar with a neck wide enough for the object to pass through.

Tie a piece of string round the object. Suspend it from the spring balance and note its weight. Fill the jar with water right up to the brim and place it in the pan on the scales. Lower the object into the water until it is submerged. The object will displace some of the water. Note the reading on the balance. Work out the change in weight of the object that has taken place. Now remove the jar and its contents from the scale pan, leaving behind the displaced water. Note the reading on the scales. What do you notice?

Floating and sinking

When you put a cork in the water, it floats. If you push it under the surface and let go, it quickly bobs to the surface again. Clearly, the water is exerting an upward force on the cork, which we call upthrust.

Any objects that are immersed in any liquids experience upthrust. A heavy object that sinks in a liquid experiences upthrust, which is what makes the object appear to lose weight.

The INVESTIGATION demonstrates that this happens. It also shows that the apparent loss in weight of an object when immersed in a liquid is equal to the weight of liquid displaced by the object. This fact was first discovered by the Greek mathematician, Archimedes over 2,000 years ago and is known as Archimedes' Principle.

When the weight of liquid displaced by an object equals the weight of that object, then it will float. This law of flotation is used in basic ship design.

▶ The *Queen Mary*, one of the best known of all transatlantic passenger liners. Measuring 310.6 metres long and launched in 1936, it is now moored at Long Beach, California, as a tourist attraction.

◄ A modern airship, often used as an aerial platform to carry TV crews. It is filled with helium gas, which is much lighter than the air it displaces. The surrounding air thus exerts an upthrust, which overcomes the airship's weight.

? 1. The first airships were filled with hydrogen gas, which is even lighter than helium. So why do airship designers now use helium?

Floating steel

The aircraft carrier USS *Nimitz* (shown right) is built of steel and weighs over 82,500 tonnes. Yet it floats. This is because the hull is designed to displace a volume of water weighing the same as the ship while the upper part of the ship is still out of the water.

What this means is that the overall density of the ship is less than the density of water. This is a more complicated way of saying that light objects float.

Archimedes' Principle and the law of flotation also apply to gases, including air. Balloons and airships will rise in the air when they displace a greater weight of air than their own weight.

The Plimsoll Line

This is the Plimsoll Line, which is marked on a ship's hull. It shows the highest water line at which the ship may safely float under different conditions. **T** stands for tropical, **F** for freshwater, **S** for summer, **W** for winter, **N** for north, **A** for Atlantic.

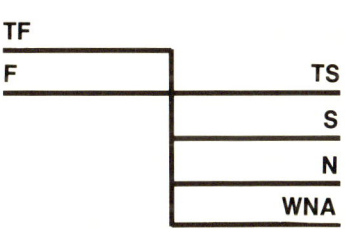

? 2. Why would it be dangerous if in January a ship took on cargo at Liverpool so that it sank to the TF line, and then sailed south to Brazil and up the River Amazon?

▶ **This craft skims across the surface of the ocean on a cushion of high-pressure air. It travels on water like a boat, but is driven by propellers like a plane.**

❓ **1. What do we call this kind of craft?**

You can show a basic difference between pressures in liquids and gases with a bicycle pump and a bucket of water. Push the handle of the pump right down and put the lower end of the pump under the surface of the water. Slowly pull up the handle, drawing water into the pump.

When the handle is fully up, put a finger over the hole at the bottom and take the pump out of the water. Keeping your finger firmly pressed, push down on the handle. What happens?

Empty the pump and then draw in a pumpful of air. Press your finger firmly against the hole at the bottom, and push down on the handle. What happens this time?

Pressure in gases

It is not only liquids that exert pressure (see page 30). Gases exert pressure, too. In fact, we live inside a great gas-filled dome, which we know as the atmosphere. The gas is the air we breathe.

We are not aware of it, but the air in the atmosphere exerts pressure on us – about 100,000 newtons on every square metre of the body (equal to the weight of 1 kg on every square centimetre). This adds up to a force equal to the weight of 20 tonnes over the whole body! However, we don't feel this force because it is balanced by an equal force inside us.

The figures quoted above (100,000 N/sq m, 1 kg/sq cm) refer to the average atmospheric pressure at sea level. But the pressure gets lower as you climb above sea level.

❓ **2.** Why does this happen?

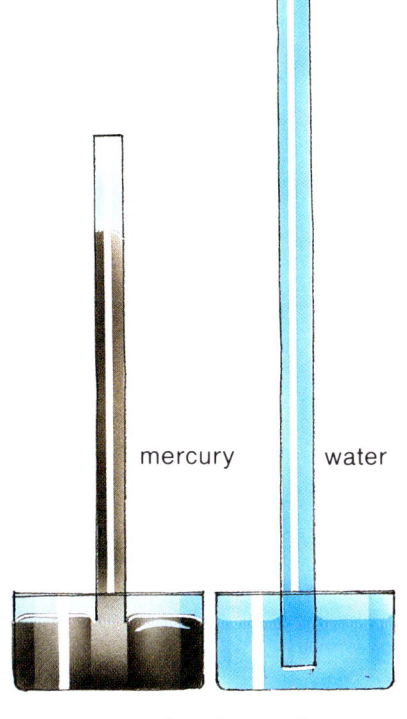

mercury   water

◀ When a long tube is filled with mercury and turned upside-down in a bowl of mercury, the mercury column in the tube drops until it stands about 76 cm above the surface.

❓ **1. (A)** What holds up the column?
(B) What kind of device is this?
(C) If you used water in the tube and bowl instead of mercury, how long would the water column be? (Mercury is 13.6 times denser than water.)

▶ Differences in air pressure across the world set the air moving, as winds. People have been harnessing wind power for centuries, as shown here in the remote outback of Australia.

Gasping for breath

As the pressure falls, or in other words as the air gets thinner, there is less oxygen to breathe. So as you climb higher, you will find that it becomes more difficult to breathe.

By the time you reach 6,000 metres, you would probably be gasping for breath. By 9,000 metres you would black out. If you somehow got to 19,000 metres, your blood would start to boil.

The air pressure even at sea level varies across the Earth's surface. Such variations give rise to massive movements of air in the atmosphere. It is the movement of air masses that bring about changes in the weather.

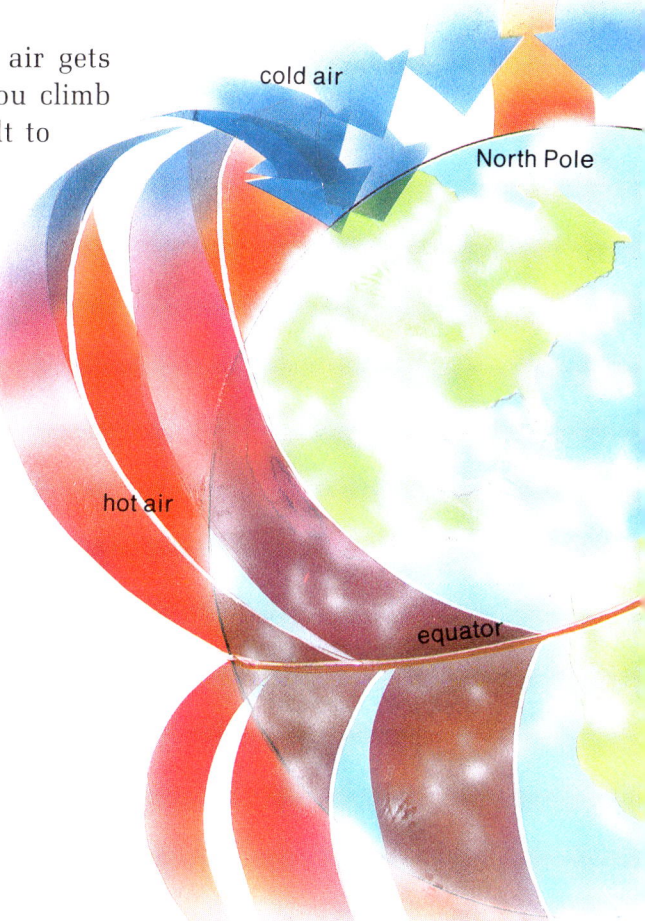

cold air

North Pole

hot air

equator

▶ The simplest air circulation in the Earth's atmosphere occurs between the Equator and the Poles. The air above the Equator rises because it is hot. The air at the Poles sinks because it is cold.

❓ **2.** Is the air pressure high or low (A) at the Equator, (B) at the Poles?

INVESTIGATE

Stick together the top and bottom edges of a sheet of paper. Hang it on a long rod or knitting needle. Now blow hard over the top. What happens?

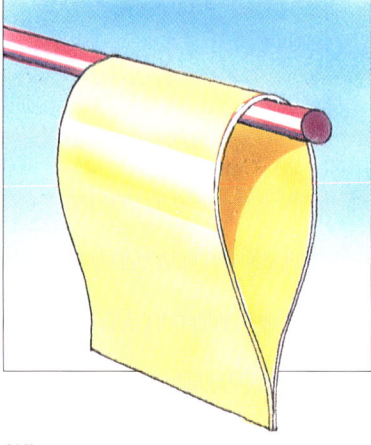

Flowing fluids

A Boeing 747 jumbo jet with a full load of passengers is very heavy – it may weigh as much as 320 tonnes. Yet it can take to the air and fly. It does so by harnessing the forces set up when bodies travel through the air. The science that deals with such forces is called aerodynamics.

Aeroplanes can fly because their wings have a special shape, called an aerofoil. An aerofoil is curved on top and flat underneath; it is broad at the front and sharp at the rear. Air flowing over the curved top of such a shape has further to go than air flowing underneath. This means that the air flowing over the top must travel faster.

Getting a lift

It is a law of aerodynamics that the pressure of a stream of air falls when it speeds up. So the faster-moving air above

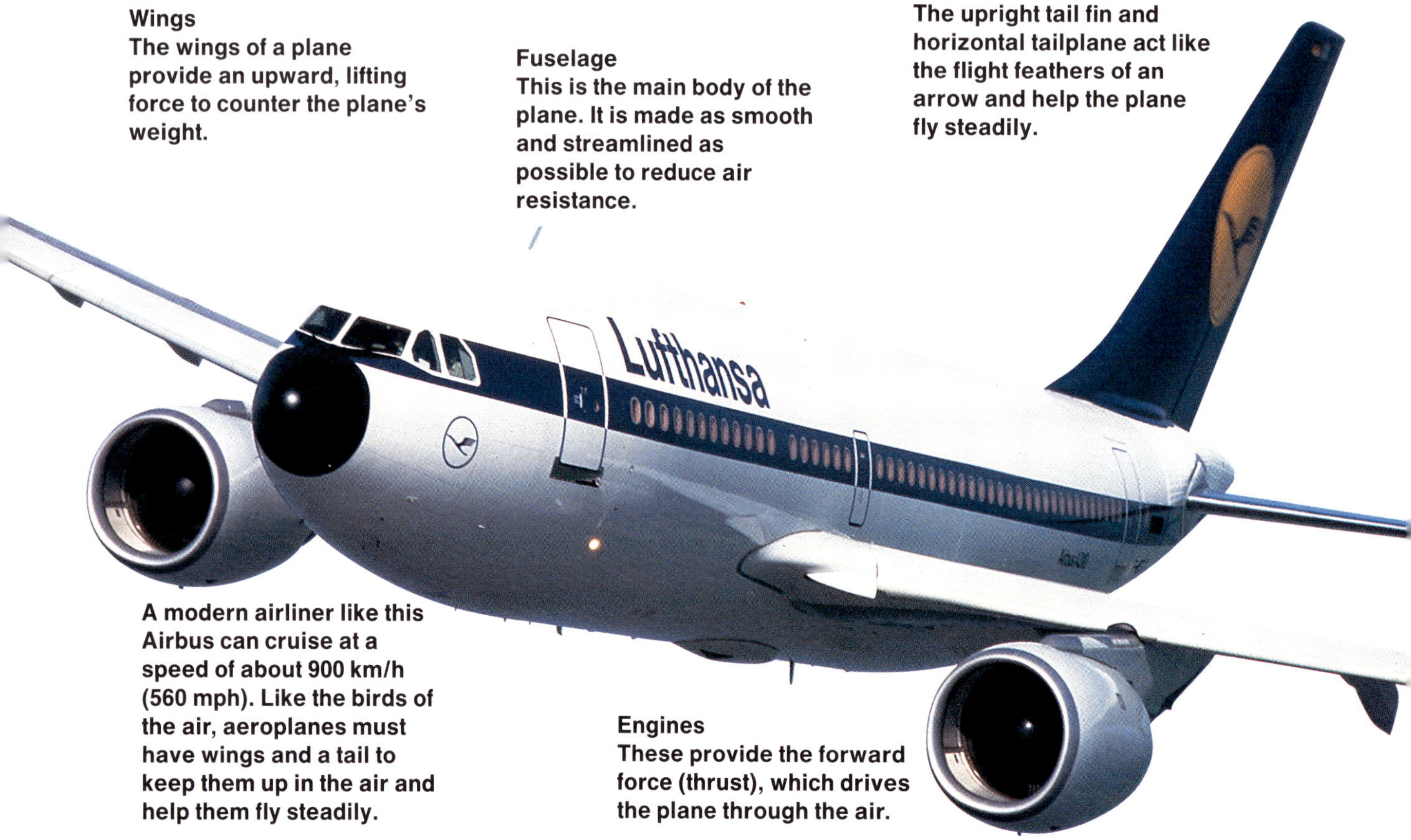

Wings
The wings of a plane provide an upward, lifting force to counter the plane's weight.

Fuselage
This is the main body of the plane. It is made as smooth and streamlined as possible to reduce air resistance.

Tail
The upright tail fin and horizontal tailplane act like the flight feathers of an arrow and help the plane fly steadily.

A modern airliner like this Airbus can cruise at a speed of about 900 km/h (560 mph). Like the birds of the air, aeroplanes must have wings and a tail to keep them up in the air and help them fly steadily.

Engines
These provide the forward force (thrust), which drives the plane through the air.

▶ Indy and Formula 1 racing cars are powerful beasts, which can reach speeds of more than 320 km/h (200 mph). At such speeds, they tend to rise in the air and fly! To keep them from doing this, they are fitted with aerofoils, or 'wings', at the front and rear.

⚇ 1. How must these wings differ from those used on planes?

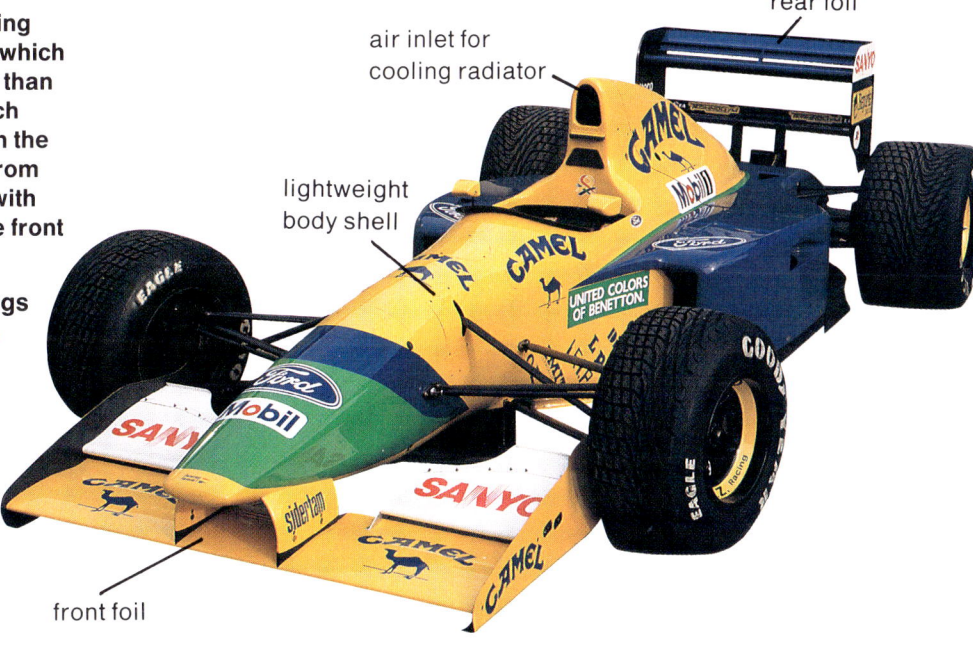

rear foil

air inlet for cooling radiator

lightweight body shell

front foil

an aerofoil must be at a lower pressure than the slower-moving air beneath it. This difference in pressure – high underneath and low on top – tends to force the aerofoil upward. It gives rise to a force we call lift. The faster the air flows past the aerofoil, the greater the lift produced.

So we can now see how to make a plane fly. We give it wings shaped like an aerofoil. We propel it along the ground faster and faster, until the wings produce more lift than the plane's weight, then the plane will leave the ground and fly.

▼ This Boeing Jetfoil is one of the most advanced hydrofoils. Powered by water jets, it cruises at over 80 km/h (50 mph).

Foils in the water

Lifting forces are also produced when similar-shaped 'wings' travel through the water. They are known as hydrofoils.

Boats fitted with hydrofoils use the lift they produce to raise the hull out of the water. Once the hull is clear of the water, it can't experience any water resistance, or drag.

⚇ 2. Why can hydrofoil boats travel much faster than ordinary ones?

▲ Designs of new cars are tested in wind tunnels to see how well they 'slip' through the air. Streams of smoke are fed into the air flow so that the flow pattern over the body can be seen and photographed.

▲ This is a sketch for a device that works because of air resistance.

❓ 1. What is it, who sketched it, and when? (A clue is 'Mona Lisa'.)

▶ This is the only successful supersonic airliner. It flies at twice the speed of sound 2,250 km/h, (1,400 mph) and twice as high as Mt. Everest.

❓ 2. What is its name? Why does it fly so high? If it leaves London at noon, what time does it arrive in Washington, 5,150 km (3,200 miles) away? (Don't forget time zones.)

◀ The fastest submarines have a bulbous-shaped hull, something like the body of a whale. It seems to be the best shape for travelling quickly through the water.

It's a drag

When objects travel through a fluid – a liquid or a gas, they experience a resisting force, which we call drag. The drag in liquids is considerable. You can't run fast when you are knee-deep in water, can you? The drag of the water holds back your legs.

The drag of gases is much less. When you are walking normally, you don't feel any air resistance. But when you ride your bicycle into a strong wind, you can feel the air resisting you. The drag increases the faster you go.

Beating drag

Aeroplanes travel at very high speeds through the air and therefore experience enormous drag. Much of the power of their engines is used to overcome this resisting force. Aircraft designers therefore take great pains to minimize drag.

An Apollo spacecraft returning from the Moon at a speed of 40,000 km/h (25,000 mph). It used air resistance as a brake to slow it down. As it entered the atmosphere, friction with the air molecules made its base glow red-hot.

They test their designs in wind tunnels, which helps them pick a streamlined shape, one that has the least drag. For supersonic planes, which travel faster than the speed of sound, the best shape is long and slender, with a 'needle' nose and well swept-back wings.

Using drag

Some flying craft, however, actively use drag to slow them down. The space shuttle, for example, relies on the drag of the atmosphere to slow it down when returning from space. It re-enters the atmosphere travelling at a speed of over 27,000 km/h (17,000 mph). About half an hour later, atmospheric drag has slowed it to a safe landing-speed.

3

The Universal Forces

◀ **Dolphins leap out of the water at Sea World in Florida, USA. But they don't keep travelling upwards because the force of gravity is pulling them back.**

Of all the forces we experience in our everyday lives, the most basic, and the most important, is gravity: the attraction, or pull, of the Earth. The force of gravity is what keeps our feet firmly on the ground and makes objects fall when they are dropped.

But gravity is not something peculiar to the Earth. It is a basic property of matter. The force of gravity acts between bodies throughout the Universe. Indeed, it is the force that literally holds the Universe together.

Gravity is a universal force that can act over very great distances. Other universal forces act strongly only over short distances. They include electromagnetism, the attraction between electrically charged and magnetic objects. But the strongest force by far occurs within the very atoms that make up matter.

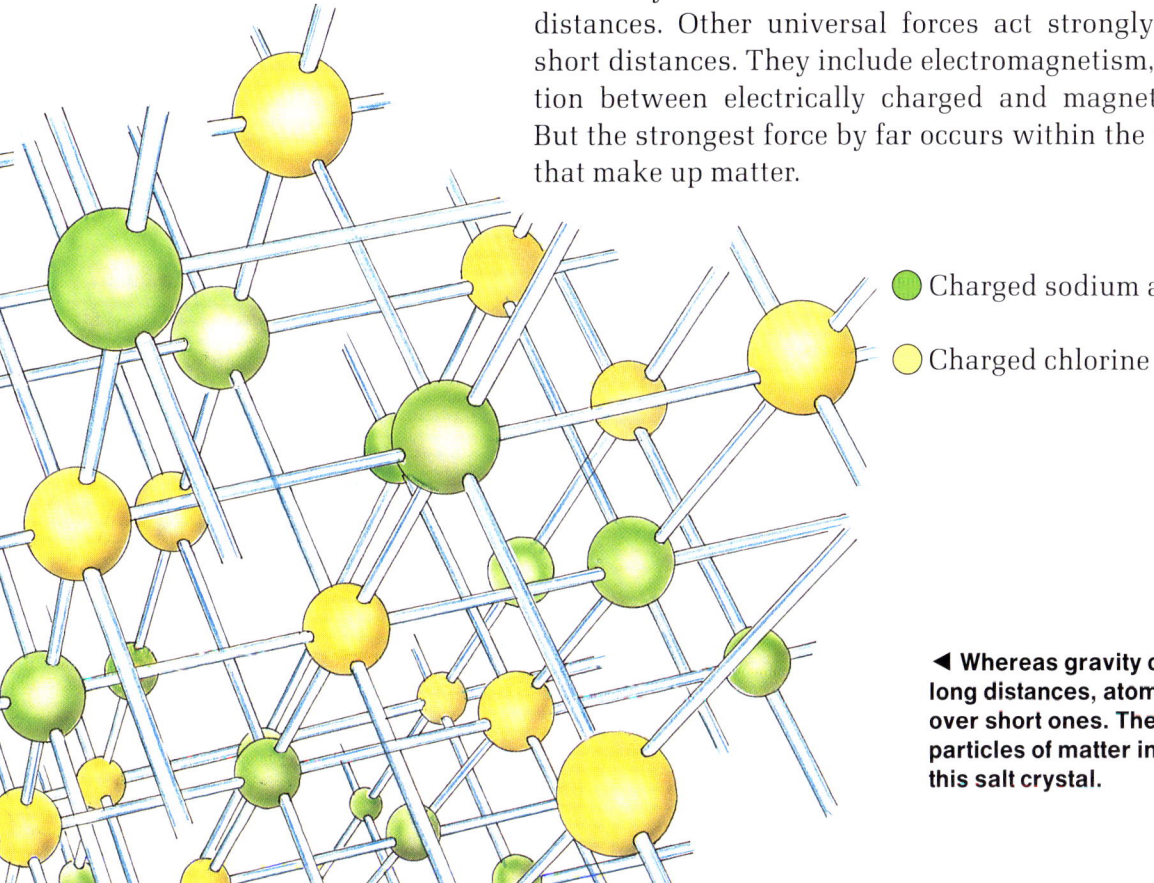

○ Charged sodium atom (+)

○ Charged chlorine atom (−)

◀ **Whereas gravity can act over long distances, atomic forces act over short ones. They keep the particles of matter in place, as in this salt crystal.**

Atomic forces

Every substance there is – flesh, rock, water and air – is made up of atoms. Atoms are the tiniest particles of a substance that can exist. Different atoms combine together to form the thousands of different substances we meet in our everyday lives.

The word 'atom' means 'that which cannot be divided'. This is not an especially good name, because scientists can now split up the atom into a number of still smaller particles, which they call subatomic particles.

Atoms are made up of three main particles – protons, neutrons and electrons. Protons and neutrons are much bigger and heavier than electrons and reside in the heart, or nucleus, of the atom. The tiny electrons circle round the nucleus.

The protons in the nucleus have a positive electric charge, and the electrons have a negative charge. The neutrons have no charge.

42

▼ **This diagram shows roughly what a typical atom is like. It has a nucleus at the centre and has a number of electrons circling round it.**

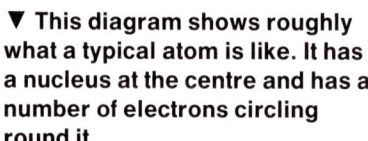 **1. The nucleus has a positive electric charge. The electrons also have an electric charge. Are they positive or negative?**

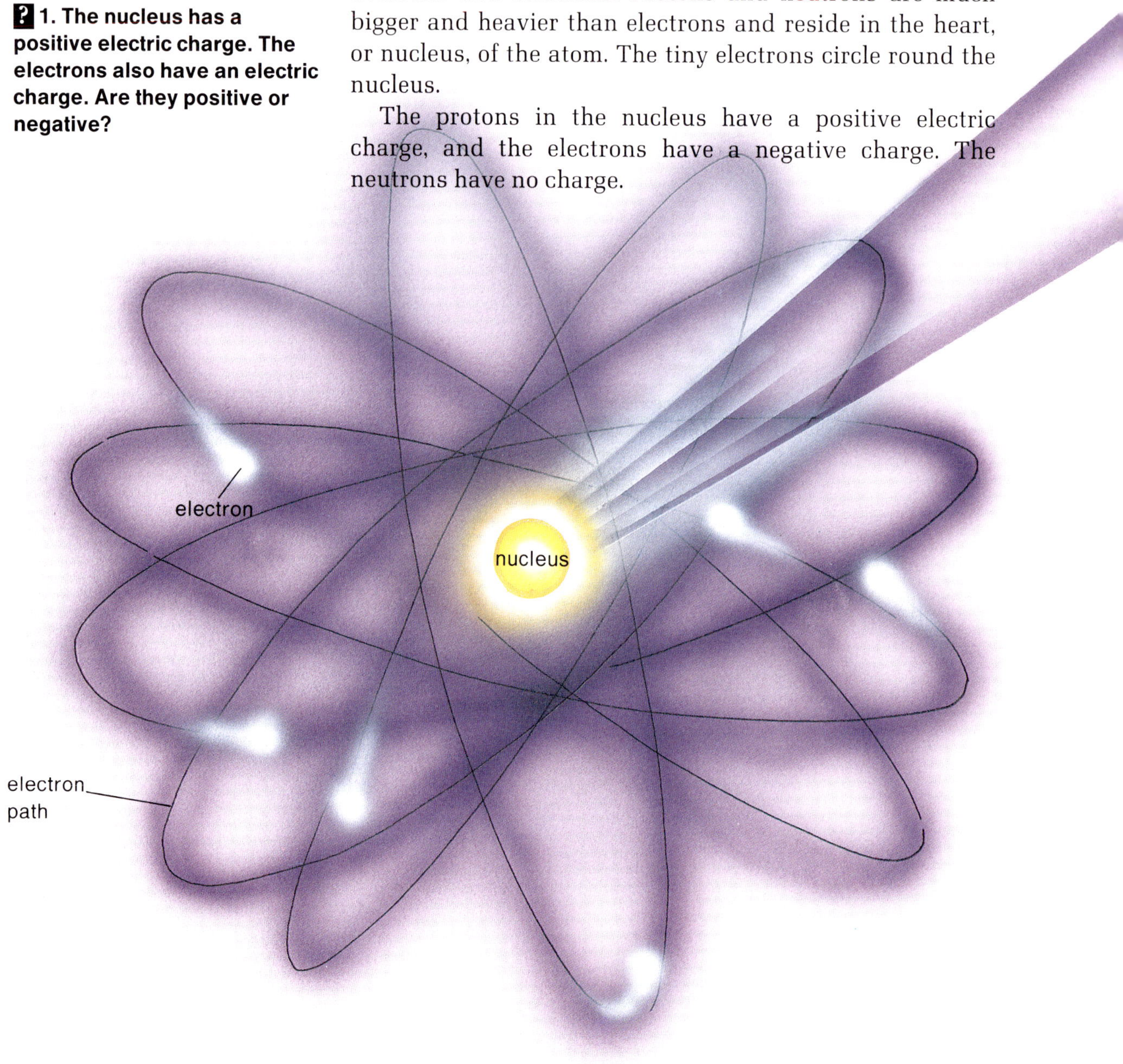

electron

nucleus

electron
path

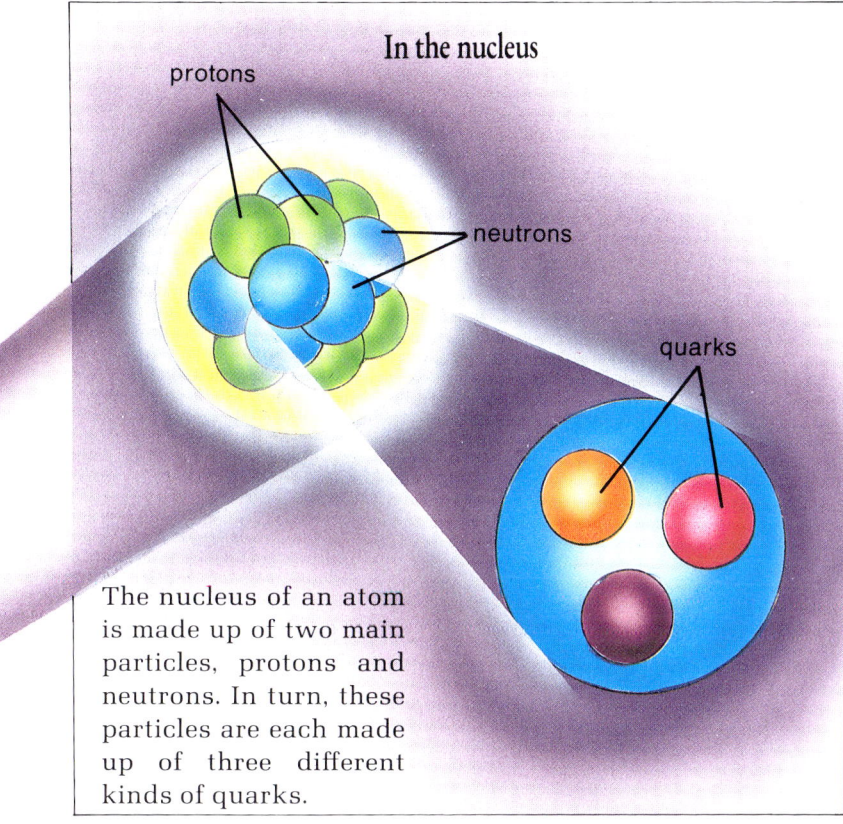

In the nucleus

protons

neutrons

quarks

The nucleus of an atom is made up of two **main** particles, protons **and** neutrons. In turn, these particles are each made up of three different kinds of quarks.

IT'S AMAZING!

One of the most mysterious particles that exists is the neutrino. It has no mass and no electric charge. All it has is energy. Neutrinos from the Sun are passing right through us all the time without having any effect.

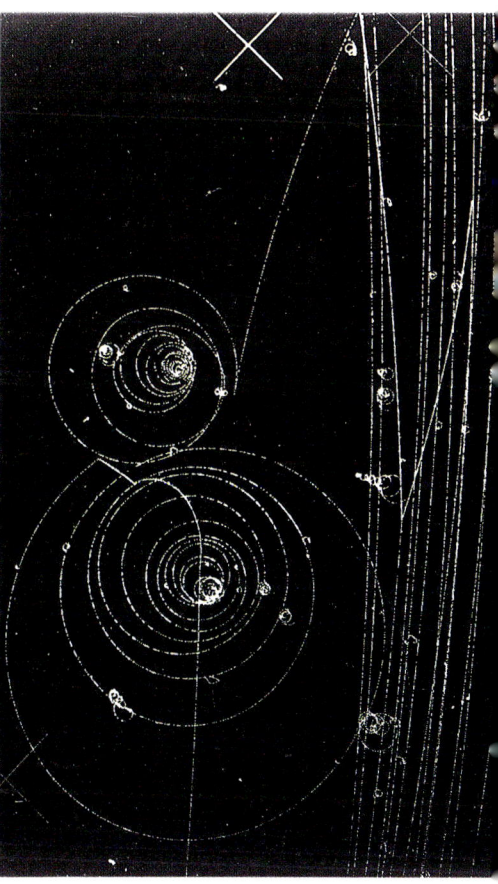

▲ A shower of subatomic particles produced in an accelerator. This machine smashes particles into one another, creating showers of new particles.

Attractive particles

It is a basic law of electricity that a positive charge attracts a negative charge. So in the atom a force of electric attraction exists between the negative electrons and the positive nucleus. It is this force that holds the atom together. Called the electromagnetic force, it is one of the basic forces of the Universe.

Another basic law of electricity is that two negative or two positive charges will repel each other. This means that in the nucleus, the positive protons must be repelling one another. Because the nucleus does not fly apart, there must exist within the nucleus a more powerful force, which binds the protons together. We call it the strong force. It is the strongest of the basic forces of the Universe, but only exists within the atom.

? The atom itself is not electrically charged. What does this tell us about the number of electrons and the number of protons in the nucleus?

44

▲ Vivid streaks of lightning stab the night sky. The streaks are produced when the air in the path of the lightning becomes white-hot.

IT'S AMAZING!

Electric charges of millions of volts build up in thunderclouds and jump to the ground as lightning strikes.

Electric and magnetic forces

In our everyday world we are not aware of the electromagnetic forces that hold atoms and molecules (groups of atoms) together (see page 43). This is because the positive and negative electric charges in the atoms balance out, leaving the atoms neutral.

However, electric charges can sometimes build up and make their presence felt, literally. If you shuffle across a nylon carpet in trainers and touch a metal door handle, you will feel a tingle in your fingers. This is because you have suffered a tiny electric shock.

As you shuffled across the carpet, you became electrically charged. Because you were wearing rubber-soled trainers, this charge couldn't get away and so built up. When you touched the handle, the electricity was able to escape, rushing out and giving you a shock.

❓ Why could the electricity escape through the handle? What would have happened if the handle had been plastic?

INVESTIGATE

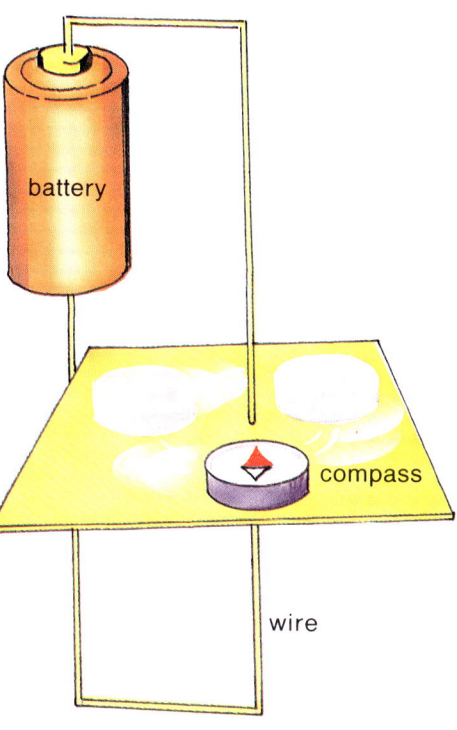

battery

compass

wire

Electricity and magnetism are closely related. Here is a way of showing this. You will need a battery, some wire, a small compass and a piece of cardboard. Set up your apparatus as shown. Complete the electric circuit by pressing the ends of the wire to the battery terminals. What happens to the compass needle? Move the compass around the cardboard, and repeat. What do you notice?

Magnetic fields

When a stream of electrically charged particles flows through a wire, we detect it as an electric current. As we see in the INVESTIGATION (left), an electric current sets up a magnetic field.

Inside atoms, the electrically charged electrons are always moving, circling round the nucleus. They therefore set up tiny magnetic fields, and the atoms in effect become tiny magnets. In most materials all these fields cancel out.

But in some materials, they don't. The tiny 'atomic magnets' align themselves in the same direction, making the whole material into a magnet. Only a handful of materials can do this, the most common being iron. Cobalt and nickel can do it too.

A magnet has its magnetism concentrated at its ends. These ends, or poles, have similar properties to electric charges. They will attract or repel one another. This is another example of the universal force we call the electromagnetic force.

▶ **The Earth behaves as if it had a huge bar magnet deep inside. Its magnetic field extends far out into space. This 'Earth magnet' has one end near the North Pole, and the other near the South Pole.**

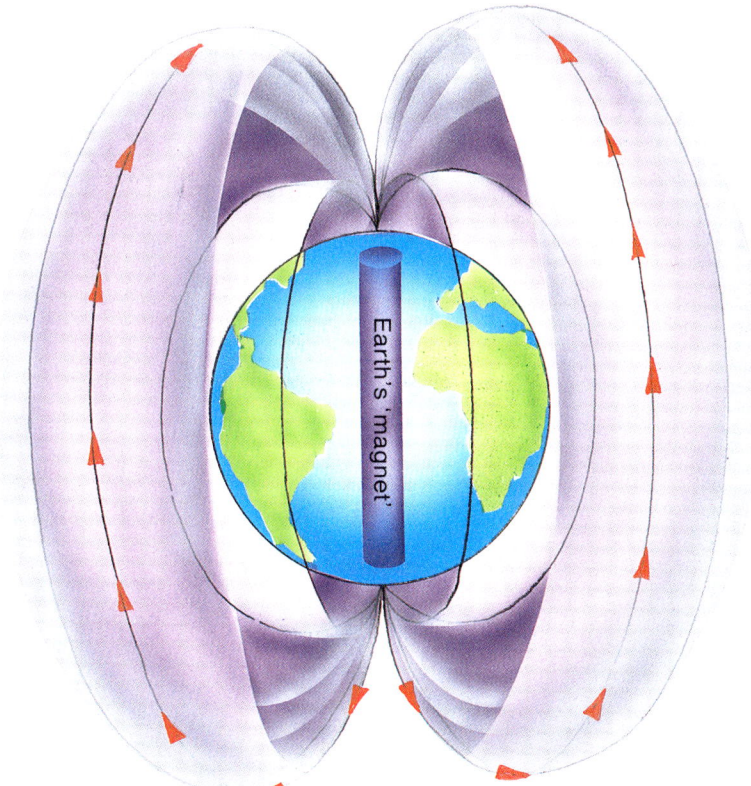

Earth's 'magnet'

Newton and the apples

One of the best-known stories in science tells of Isaac Newton's discovery of the law of gravity. It supposedly happened in about 1666, when Newton, a 'natural scientist' at Cambridge University in England, had returned home to Lincolnshire to escape the Great Plague, which was laying waste Europe at the time.

One day, so the story goes, he was watching apples dropping from a tree. It suddenly struck him that the same force that attracted the apples to the ground kept the Moon in orbit round the Earth, and that every body possessed a similar kind of attractive force, the force of gravity.

Gravity

The force of gravity is truly a universal force. It acts throughout the Universe and affects all matter – the Earth, the Moon, the Sun, the stars and the galaxies.

The English scientist Isaac Newton was the first person to realize that the pull the Earth exerts on apples – and on other objects on and near it – is a basic property of all matter (see Box, left). He worked out mathematically how this pull could be calculated.

The result was his law of universal gravitation, which we can state as follows: 'Every particle of matter attracts every other particle with a force that is proportional to the masses of the particles and inversely proportional to the square of the distance between them.'

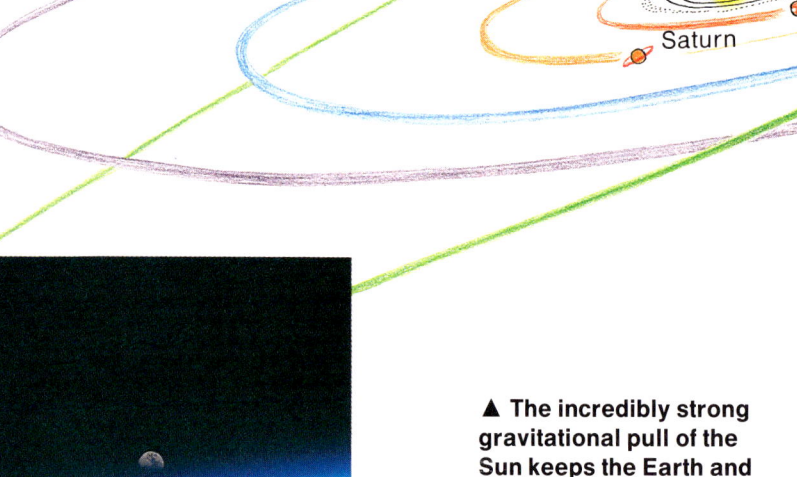

Sun

Asteroid belt

Jupiter

Saturn

▲ The incredibly strong gravitational pull of the Sun keeps the Earth and all the other planets in their orbits.

▲ The Earth's gravity holds the Moon in its grasp, even over a distance of some 395,000 km (239,000 miles).

▲ Gravity binds together the Sun and all the other stars in the night sky into a great 'star island', or galaxy. From a distance, it would look like the famous Andromeda Galaxy, pictured here.

❓ 1. Why is the Andromeda Galaxy so famous?

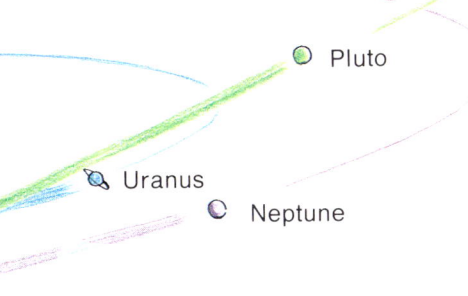

Pluto

Uranus

Neptune

Gravity among the stars

Gravity affects how stars are born, live and die. A star is born when gravity makes a cloud of gas and dust start to collapse. As it collapses, the cloud releases gravitational energy, just as a ball releases energy when it falls to the ground.

In the collapsing cloud, the energy is released as heat. The more it collapses, the hotter it gets. In time, it becomes hot enough to trigger off nuclear reactions, which release fantastic energy as radiation. The outward flow of this radiation prevents the gas cloud from collapsing further, and it becomes a steadily shining body we call a star.

Gravity also affects how a star dies. When a small star like the Sun dies, gravity makes it slowly shrink into a tiny white dwarf star. But when the bigger stars die they blast themselves apart. The matter that remains collapses under gravity to form tiny and very dense bodies.

IT'S AMAZING!

When a very big star dies, its matter is crushed into a tiny region of space. In that region gravity is so intense nothing, not even light, can escape from it. We call it a black hole.

❓ 2. Why is 'black hole' a good name for it?

Falling bodies

We can learn much about gravity on Earth by studying the way in which objects fall to the ground. An Italian scientist named Galileo was one of the first people to investigate falling bodies about 400 years ago.

Galileo is supposed to have conducted an experiment at the famous Leaning Tower in Pisa, the city in which he lived. In about 1590 he dropped two cannonballs of different weights from the top of the Tower and observed what happened.

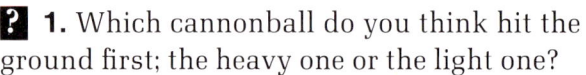

? **1.** Which cannonball do you think hit the ground first; the heavy one or the light one?

▶ Skydivers fall quickly when they jump from their plane thousands of metres above the Earth. Gravity tugs at their bodies and makes them travel faster and faster.

? **2.** The maximum speed they reach is called the terminal velocity. What speed is it: 160, 240, 320, 400, 480 km/h (100, 150, 200, 250, 300 mph)?

INVESTIGATE

Find two identical empty plastic containers with lids. Leave one empty, but fill the other with sand so it is much heavier. Hold up the two tubs at the same height, and let them go at the same time. Which tub hits the floor first?

Repeat the experiment with other pairs of similar-sized objects of different weights, such as a golf ball and a ping-pong ball, or an orange and a ball of wool. What do you find? Why do you think it is important to use pairs of objects of similar size?

▶ The famous Leaning Tower of Pisa, in the city of Pisa, Italy. It leans over at such an angle that an object dropped from the top would land 5 metres from the base.

? **3.** Why was this a good place for Galileo to conduct his cannonball experiment?

A basic law

Before you carried out the last INVESTIGATION, you might have thought that the heavier objects of each pair would hit the ground first simply because they were heavier. But they didn't, did they? Both the light and the heavy objects hit the ground together.

This illustrates a basic law of falling bodies: under the influence of gravity alone, bodies fall to the ground at the same rate.

Breaking the law

Does this law of falling bodies always apply? What happens if you drop an orange and a sheet of paper together? Do they hit the floor together? No, they don't. The orange drops straight down quickly, but the paper takes its time, wafting lazily from side to side.

Why does the paper fall more slowly? Clearly, another force besides gravity must be at work. It is – air resistance. This is the force the air exerts on anything moving through it. The sheet of paper presents a bigger area to the air as it falls, and so it experiences greater air resistance and falls more slowly. (Read more about air resistance on page 34.)

? 1. How can you make the sheet of paper fall at the same rate as the orange?

The spaceman ... the hammer ... and the feather

In July 1971 an Apollo astronaut named David Scott carried out an experiment on the Moon. He dropped a hammer and a feather from the same height and found that they hit the surface at the same time. 'How about that,' cried Scott, 'Mr Galileo was correct!'

? 2. What did David Scott mean?

The essential workings of a pendulum clock, which is powered and regulated by gravity.

❓ How is it powered and regulated by gravity? The investigation below should help you.

INVESTIGATE

Make a simple pendulum from a length of thread with a steel nut tied to one end. Hang it up and set it swinging. Time how long it takes to swing from side to side. (It is best to time 10 swings and divide by 10.) Alter the length of the thread and repeat. What do you find?

The g-force

If we ignore air resistance, the basic law of gravity holds: all bodies fall to the Earth at the same rate. In other words, they gain speed at the same rate.

Suppose you dropped a pebble over a cliff and could measure its speed as it fell. Before it started to fall, of course, its speed would be zero. After it had been falling one second, you would find it would be moving at a speed of about 10 metres per second.

After another second, it would be moving another 10 metres per second faster, at 20 metres per second; and after another second, 30 metres per second; and so on. It would continue gaining speed at the rate of 10 metres per second until it hit the ground.

Acceleration due to gravity

We call the rate at which a body gains speed its acceleration. So the acceleration the pebble experiences, due to the pull of gravity, is 10 metres per second per second. All bodies falling to the Earth experience this same acceleration due to gravity, which we call g. But on other heavenly bodies, g is different (see opposite page).

Mass and weight

On Earth, the force of gravity acts on every object, trying to pull it down. Because of gravity we call the amount of force acting downwards on an object its weight.

From Newton's law of gravity (see page 46), we know that the amount of the gravitational force depends on the mass of the object. In other words, the weight of an object depends on its mass. In fact, the object's weight equals it's mass multiplied by g (see page 10).

The terms 'mass' and 'weight' are often confused, but as you can see, they are quite different. 'Mass' is the amount of matter in a body. 'Weight' is the amount of force acting on it because of gravity. In everyday life, we usually talk about pound and kilogram weights. But strictly speaking, these units refer to masses rather than weights.

◀ On the Moon, the Apollo astronauts wore bulky spacesuits and backpacks and carried heavy equipment. Yet they could move around easily.

? **1. Why?**

High gs and low gs

We have seen that the weight of an object equals its mass times g. In turn, g depends on the mass of the attracting body. The more massive the attracting body, the greater its g is. The Moon is much smaller and has much less mass than the Earth. Its g is only one-sixth that of the Earth. Jupiter is much bigger and much more massive than the Earth. Its g is 2.54 times that of the Earth.

? **2.** If an object weighs 1,000 N on Earth, how much would it weigh on the Moon? On Jupiter? Give your answers in newtons.

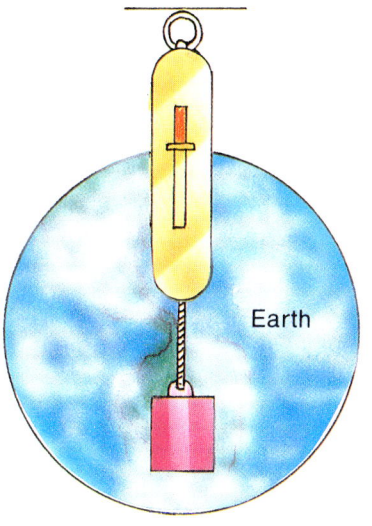

Earth

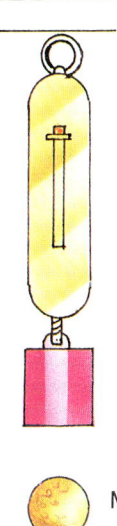

Moon

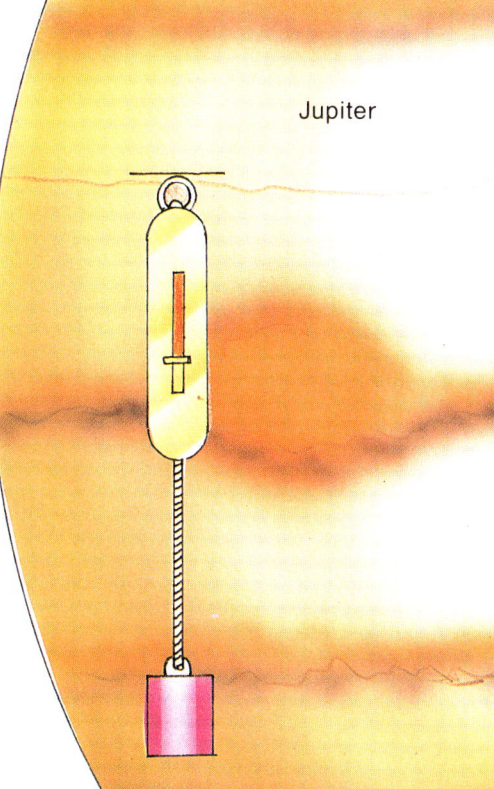

Jupiter

52

Beating gravity

The Earth's force of gravity is very powerful. It keeps our feet on the ground, the water in the oceans, and the air in the atmosphere. In our everyday experience, what goes up must come down. So how can we overcome gravity and launch bodies into space?

Imagine you are playing cricket and are batting. When you hit the ball, you make it move fast, and it travels some way before gravity pulls it back to the ground. The harder you hit the ball, the faster it moves, and the further it travels before falling back to the ground. This gives us a clue about how we can beat gravity – by speed.

Getting into orbit

Now imagine that you can hit the cricket ball as hard as you like. As you hit it harder and harder, it travels faster and faster, and further and further, before it falls back to the ground.

A strange thing happens when you hit the ball at a speed of 28,000 km/h (17,500 mph). At that speed it travels a very long way, falling slowly. The amount that it falls equals the amount that the Earth's surface falls away beneath it. In other words, it stays the same height above the ground.

▲ The Hubble Space Telescope was placed in orbit by the space shuttle in 1990. It looks deep into space to spy on the planets and the stars.

? 2. The large panels on either side are not used to reflect sunlight and keep the telescope from getting too hot. What are they used for?

If there were nothing to slow it down, the ball would continue to circle the Earth indefinitely. It would become a satellite in orbit round the Earth.

Space satellites

In practice, we don't launch satellites by hitting them with a cricket bat! We use a rocket to boost them to the necessary speed of 28,000 km/h (17,500 mph) to get them into orbit. We call this speed the orbital velocity.

We have to launch satellites so that they circle above the Earth's atmosphere. Otherwise air resistance will slow them down, and then gravity will be able to pull them down to Earth again.

Up in orbit, as we mentioned earlier, everything is falling but staying the same height above the ground. We call this condition 'free fall'. The popular term for it is weightlessness, because nothing in orbit appears to have any weight.

IT'S AMAZING!

A small satellite called Lageos was launched into orbit in 1976. It will not fall back to Earth for 10 million years. By then the shape of the continents will have changed markedly.

❓ 1. Why?

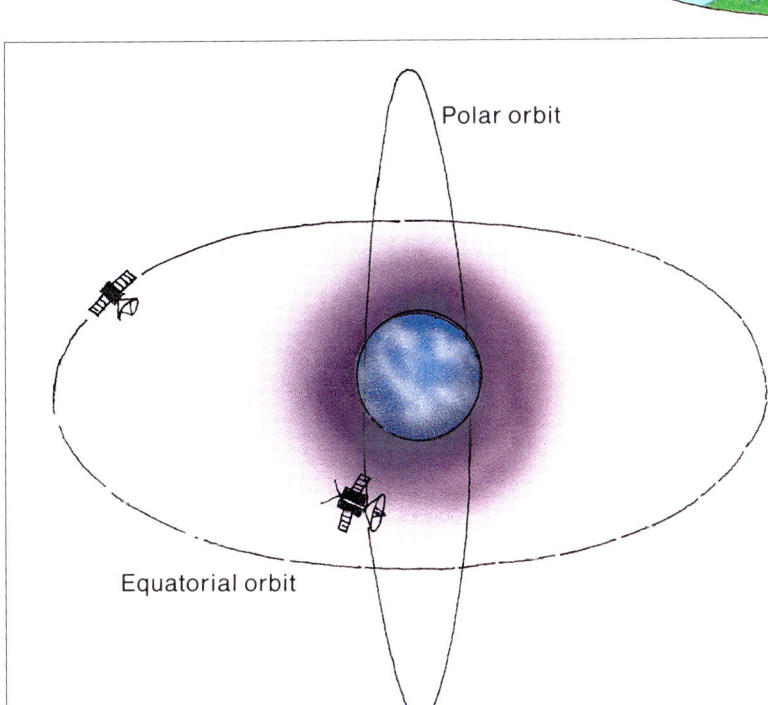

Polar orbit

Equatorial orbit

Satellite orbits

Satellites are launched into various orbits around the Earth. Many weather satellites are launched into a polar orbit, passing over the North and South Poles. Many communications satellites are launched into an equatorial orbit above the Equator. They circle at a height of about 36,000 km (22,300 miles).

❓ 2. A satellite at that height travels at a speed of 11,060 km/h (6,870 mph). How long does it take to circle the Earth? The Earth's diameter is 12,756 km (7,926 miles).

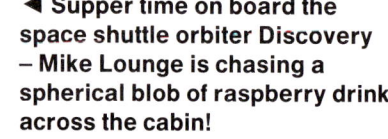

◀ Supper time on board the space shuttle orbiter Discovery – Mike Lounge is chasing a spherical blob of raspberry drink across the cabin!

? 2. Why would it not be a good idea for astronauts to shake pepper on their food?

▲ Astronauts snooze in their bunks on the mid-deck of the shuttle orbiter. Note the way their arms float in the air.

? 3. When they retire to bed, astronauts zip themselves into bags called sleeping restraints. Why do you think they are called 'restraints'?

Zero-g

If you become an astronaut and ride the space shuttle into orbit, you will find living there a novel experience. On Earth, you are used to having a body that has weight and doing things in the presence of gravity. But up in orbit you are weightless. There appears to be no gravity, a state we call zero-g.

So what is life like in the weightless, zero-g world in orbit? To start with, you can't walk, because there is nothing to keep your feet down on the floor. You have to pull or push yourself along.

You can eat normally with a fork and spoon, as long as you move them slowly. Move them quickly, and your food could shoot into someone else's mouth! However, you can't drink normally. You have to suck liquids through a straw or squirt them into your mouth.

? 1. Why can't you pour yourself a glass of milk in orbit?

You and you body

On the space shuttle you will find plenty of water for drinking and washing. But don't use too much water for washing, otherwise water droplets will scatter all over the place and give your fellow astronauts a bath, too!

Zero-g also presents a problem when you go to the lavatory. On Earth, body wastes fall away under gravity when they leave the body. In zero-g, they just hang around! Fortunately, the shuttle has a flushing system that solves the problem. The flushing is not done by water as it is on Earth, but by a stream of air. Another unusual feature of the space lavatory is that it has a seat belt!

If you want to exercise on the shuttle, you can jog on a treadmill. This helps keep your muscles from wasting away.

? **1.** Why do muscles start to waste away in zero-g?

55

▼ In the weightless conditions of space, you can carry out impressive feats, like balancing a fellow astronaut on your finger!

? **2.** What happens if you take your finger away?

▲ Juggling in orbit is child's play – if you cheat. All you need do is place the objects in mid-air and pretend!

Milestones

ABOUT 2000 BC Architects in Mesopotamia (modern Iraq) understood the load-bearing principles of the arch, used to perfection 2,000 years later by Roman engineers to build bridges and aqueducts.

200s BC The Greek Archimedes studied the floating and sinking of objects and stated the principle named after him. He also developed the law of the lever.

1232 The first documented use of rockets by the Chinese in their war against the Mongols.

1584 Galileo in Italy discovered the law of the pendulum.

ABOUT 1590 Galileo proved his law of falling bodies by dropping cannonballs from the top of the Leaning Tower of Pisa.

1643 Evangelista Torricelli in Italy invented the barometer.

circa MID-1600s Blaise Pascal in France discovered the law of hydraulics named after him: that a liquid transmits pressure equally in all directions.

1666 Isaac Newton in England was inspired (so it is said) by a falling apple to develop the law of gravity.

1687 Isaac Newton published his laws of motion and gravity in one of the most important science books ever written, the *Principia*.

MID-1700s Daniel Bernoulli in Switzerland discovered the law named after him: that the higher the speed of a gas, the lower is its pressure.

1884-5 The 10-storey Home Insurance Building in Chicago became the first building to be built with a load-bearing metal frame. It was the ancestor of the modern skyscraper.

1901 The Wright brothers built a wind tunnel to test the aerodynamics of aircraft wings, which led to their development of the first powered plane.

1910 The Dutch physicist Johannes van der Waals was awarded the Nobel Prize in physics for his work on the behaviour of liquids and gases. He described how their behaviour is affected by the forces between the molecules, often called van der Waals forces.

1931 The 102-storey Empire State Building was completed in New York City. With a total height of nearly 450 metres, it remained the world's tallest building until 1970.

1945 In July, a B-25 bomber crashed with tremendous force into the Empire State Building. But because of its very strong structure, the building suffered only minor damage.

1957 A Russian rocket launched Sputnik 1, the first man-made object to beat Earth's gravity and climb into space.

1960 Jacques Piccard and Donald Walsh made the deepest ever ocean descent in the bathyscaphe *Trieste*. They dived into Challenger Deep in the Pacific, reaching a depth of 10,916 metres (35,813 feet).

1968 In December, the crew of Apollo 8 became the first humans to escape Earth's gravity and be captured by the gravity of another world, the Moon.

1990 Scientists discovered a third new form of carbon with a dome-like structure called buckminsterfullerene after a famous US architect.

Glossary

ACCELERATION The rate at which the speed/velocity of a moving body changes.

AERODYNAMICS The study of the forces involved when a body travels through the air.

AEROFOIL The cross-sectional shape of an aeroplane's wing, which develops a lifting force when it travels through the air.

ARCHIMEDES' PRINCIPLE The apparent loss in weight of a body when immersed in a fluid is equal to the weight of fluid displaced.

ATMOSPHERIC PRESSURE The pressure the air in the atmosphere exerts on everything on Earth.

ATOM The smallest particle of a chemical element that still has the properties of that element.

CENTRE OF MASS/CENTRE OF GRAVITY An imaginary point in a body at which all the mass/weight of the body appears to be concentrated.

CENTRIPETAL FORCE A force on a body moving in a circle, directed towards the centre of the circle.

CHEMICAL ELEMENTS The 'building blocks' of matter; the basic substances from which all matter is made up.

DRAG The resisting force bodies experience when they move through a gas or a liquid, particularly through air or water.

ELECTRIC CHARGE A unit of electricity, carried by nuclear particles, such as electrons and protons. Charges can be positive or negative. Two charges exert a force on each other: unlike charges attract, like charges repel.

ELECTROMAGNETIC FORCE The force that arises when two electric charges or magnetic poles are brought near each other. Electromagnetic forces hold the atom together.

ELECTRON One of the basic particles of matter, with a negative electric charge. In atoms, a number of electrons circle around a central nucleus.

ELEMENTS See CHEMICAL ELEMENTS.

EQUILIBRIUM A state in which a body or a system will remain unless disturbed by an outside force.

FRICTION A force that affects moving bodies and opposes their motion. It is set up when one surface rubs against another.

G The acceleration due to gravity, that is, the acceleration a body experiences when falling under gravity.

GRAVITY The force with which the Earth pulls everything on or near it. More generally, the force of attraction that exists between any lumps of matter anywhere in the Universe.

HYDRAULIC PRESSURE Liquid pressure.

INCLINED PLANE A 'simple machine', consisting essentially of a slope.

INERTIA A basic property of matter, which makes a body try to remain in the same state as it is: for a body that is stationary to remain stationary, and for a moving body to keep on moving in the same direction and at the same speed.

JET ENGINE An engine that works on the reaction principle. The force developed by a jet of gases streaming backwards sets up a reaction force forwards, which propels the engine.

KINETIC THEORY A theory that explains the basic nature and behaviour of matter. It says that matter is composed of particles in motion.

LEVER A 'simple machine', consisting essentially of a rod that turns round, or turns on a pivot – or fulcrum.

MACHINE A device for doing useful work – one in which a force (effort) applied at one point is used to overcome a force (load) at another.

MAGNETISM A property of iron and a few other metals that enables them to attract or repel similar metals. It is closely related to static electricity, the electricity relating to electric charges, and obeys a similar law: that unlike magnetic poles attract, like poles repel. See also ELECTRIC CHARGE.

MASS A measure of the amount of matter in a substance, expressed in units such as kilograms or pounds.

MATTER The 'stuff' from which substances are made up.

MOLECULE The smallest unit of a substance that can exist by itself. It consists of a number of atoms of the same or of different elements bonded together.

MOMENTUM A property possessed by a moving body, being the mass multiplied by the velocity.

NEUTRON A particle found in the nucleus of all atoms except the lightest, hydrogen. As its name suggests, it has no electric charge.

NEWTON (N) A standard international unit of force widely used in science. It is the force that would give a mass of 1 kilogram an acceleration of 1 metre per second per second.

NUCLEUS The central part of an atom, which has most of the atom's mass. It is made up of two main particles, protons and neutrons.

ORBIT The path of a satellite round the Earth, or the path of one heavenly body round another.

ORBITAL VELOCITY The speed at which a satellite must travel to remain in orbit.

PENDULUM A device consisting of a rod or thread with a weight at the end, that swings back and forth.

POLES The regions at the ends of a magnet in which the magnetism appears to be concentrated.

PRESSURE The force acting on a unit area of surface, measured in units such as newtons per square metre, kilograms per square centimetre and pounds per square inch.

PROTON A particle found in the nucleus of all atoms. It has a positive electric charge. See also ELECTRON, NEUTRON.

REACTION PRINCIPLE The name often given to Newton's third law of motion: to every action there is an equal and opposite reaction.

ROCKET An engine that works on the reaction principle. The force of gases rushing out backwards from the engine sets up a force forwards (called thrust), which propels the rocket.

STREAMLINED The special shape of a body that enables it to experience the least resistance when moving through a fluid.

SUBATOMIC PARTICLES Particles that are smaller than the atom, many of which reside in the atom.

SUPERSONIC Faster than the speed of sound.

SURFACE TENSION A downward force that exists at the surface of a liquid, which makes the liquid appear to have a 'skin'.

TENSILE STRENGTH The strength of a body when it is subjected to tensile (stretching) forces.

VECTOR A mathematical quantity that has direction as well as magnitude. Velocity is a vector.

VELOCITY The speed of a body in a certain direction.

WEIGHT The force acting on a body because of the downward pull of gravity. In everyday life, weight is usually expressed in units of mass, such as kilograms and pounds. In science, weight is usually expressed in the force units called newtons.

WEIGHTLESSNESS The condition astronauts experience in orbit when they and everything else appears to have no weight.

WHEEL AND AXLE A 'simple machine': a winch is an example. The load is supported by a rope running over the axle. The axle is turned by a large wheel or crank at one end.

WORK A measure of the energy put into or taken out of a machine or system. It is associated with movement. Work done equals force multiplied by distance.

ZERO-G An alternative name for weightlessness.

Answers

Page 10
Two balls would swing up on the other side.

Page 11
Investigate
As the cork pops out forwards, the bottle shoots backwards. This follows from Newton's third law.

Page 12
Tricky questions
Draughts: You can take out the bottom draught by knocking it sharply with a ruler. The inertia of the rest of the draughts in the pile keeps them together.

Eggs: Spin both eggs rapidly, then stop them. The hard boiled egg keeps still, but the raw egg starts moving again. This is because the liquid inside the shell keeps moving, because of its inertia.

Page 13
1. In a drive, the golf ball experiences mainly air resistance, or drag. In a putt, the ball is slowed down mainly by friction with the grass.
2. Perpetual-motion machines can never be built because they all suffer from friction between their moving parts, which sooner or later will stop them from moving.

Page 14
Workout
George lives at Navaronne; Karen lives at Monica Falls; Emma lives at Calamity Gulch; Bill lives at Cheyenne Pass; Dawn lives at Big Rock. You take 36 minutes to reach George's house; 48 minutes to Karen's; 1 hour to Emma's; 54 minutes to Bill's and Dawn's.

Page 15
Workout
The boat ends up travelling at a speed of (**A**) 19 km/h (12 mph) in a north easterly direction.
(**B**) 41 km/h (26 mph) in a north easterly direction.

Page 17
This toy has a heavy weight at the bottom, and therefore a low centre of mass (or gravity). When the toy is not upright, its centre of mass always exerts a turning force around the pivoting point. This turning force acts to return the toy to the upright position.

Page 21
An effort-force of only 25 newtons would be required to lift the 100 newtons. Only one quarter of the load-force is needed because the rope has been pulled out four times as far as the load has been lifted.

Page 23
1. The Concorde is travelling at twice the speed of sound, at 2,200 km/h (1,367 mph). So relative to the ground, Fred is moving at 2,208 km/h (1,372 mph).
2. In 24 hours, a point on the ground near the Equator travels a distance equal to the Earth's circumference ($\pi \times$ diameter). Its speed is 1,675 km/h (1,041 mph). Let's assume for this calculation that the Concorde starts out near the Equator. So Fred is moving round the Earth's axis at a speed of 3,883 km/h (2,413 mph).
3. In 365 days the Earth travels the length of its orbit ($2 \times \pi \times$ the distance of the Earth from the Sun). The Earth's speed in orbit is 107,294 km/h. Fred is circling in orbit round the Sun at a speed of 111,174 km/h .
4. The Sun takes 250 million years to travel the length of its orbit round the Galaxy

($2 \times \pi \times$ distance from the centre). The Sun's speed around the centre is 830,663 km/h. Fred therefore circles round the centre of the Galaxy at 941,839 km/h.

5. 90 per cent of the speed of light is 972,000,000 km/h. So Fred is moving relative to the quasars at 972,941,839 km/h.

Page 27

1. The water rises up the tube, again because of the attraction between the glass and water molecules.

2. The pond skater 'walks' on the surface skin of the water.

Investigate

The other force involved is air pressure, which acts against the film of water trapped in the mesh of the sieve.

Page 28

1. The force of gravity causes the concrete slab to sag in the middle.

2. The two main natural forms of carbon are graphite, a rather soft material and, diamond, which is the hardest material there is.

Page 29

The Golden Gate is a suspension bridge.

Page 30

1. The Hoover Dam is built across the Colorado River. The reservoir is Lake Mead.

2. The dam has to be very thick at the bottom to withstand the great water pressure there.

Investigate

From this experiment we can see that the force making the water spurt out must increase as the water depth increases.

Page 31

Workout

A. Challenger Deep is about 11,000 metres deep.

B. It is 1.76 times deeper than Mt. McKinley

is high; and 1.23 times deeper than Mt. Everest is high.

C. The pressure at the bottom of Challenger Deep is about 1,100 times normal atmospheric pressure, or about 110,000,000 Pa.

Page 33

1. Hydrogen forms an explosive mixture with air. Many early airships caught fire or exploded for this reason. Helium is not flammable: it does not burn.

2. As the ship sailed south, the temperature of the sea water would rise. It would therefore become less dense. So the ship would have to sink lower in the water to displace a greater volume of water to equal its own weight. As the ship sailed into the Amazon, it would sink even lower because freshwater is less dense than seawater. It could be that the ship would then sink dangerously low in the water.

Page 34

1. This surface-skimming craft is called an air-cushion vehicle. Another more common name for it is hovercraft.

2. The pressure of the atmosphere decreases as you climb upwards, because there is less air above you to press down.

Page 35

1. (**A**) Air pressure holds up the column of mercury.

(**B**) The device is called a barometer.

(**C**) The column of water would be 10.4 metres long.

2. (**A**) At the Equator the air pressure is low because the air is warm and rising.

(**B**) At the Poles the air pressure is high because the air is cold and sinking.

Page 36

Investigate

By sticking together the edges of the sheet of

paper, you have shaped it into an aerofoil. When you blow over the top, you find it will rise. This is because you have lowered the air pressure above it, which causes the ordinary air pressure underneath to push it up.

Page 37
1. The 'wings' fitted to a racing car must be the other way up, so that when air flows past them, they push down rather than lift up as they do on a plane.
2. Water resistance on the hull is the main thing that makes ordinary boats so slow. With their hull out of the water, hydrofoils experience little resistance and can thus travel much faster.

Page 38
1. This is a sketch of a primitive parachute, a device that works because of air resistance. It was drawn by the Italian artist Leonardo da Vinci in the late 1400s. He painted the 'Mona Lisa', with her haunting smile, in about 1505.
2. This supersonic airliner is the Concorde, which is of British and French design. It flies high, where the air is thin, so it experiences less drag. If the Concorde leaves London at noon, it should arrive in Washington at about 9.30 am.

Page 42
The electrons have a negative charge. Electrical attraction binds them to the positively charged nucleus.

Page 43
There are equal numbers of protons and electrons in an atom.

Page 44
The electricity could escape through the door handle because it was made of metal, and metals conduct electricity. If the handle had been plastic, you wouldn't have felt a shock. This is because plastics don't conduct electricity: they are insulators.

Page 45
Investigate
When you switch on the current, the compass needle will move, because the current has set up a magnetic field. If you move the compass in a circle around the card, you will find that it always points in the direction in which you are moving.

Page 47
1. The Andromeda Galaxy is famous because it is the farthest object we can see with the naked eye. It lies some 2.3 million light-years away, or about 23 million million kilometres (14 million million miles).
2. Black hole is a good name for this mysterious object because no light can escape from it.

Page 48
1. Both cannonballs hit the ground at the same time.
2. Skydivers reach a terminal velocity of about 320 km/h (200 mph).
3. Because the Tower of Pisa leans, the cannonballs were able to fall freely without hitting the Tower walls.

Page 49
1. You can make the paper fall at the same rate as the orange by crushing it up into a ball.
2. David Scott proved Galileo's law of falling bodies. On Earth air resistance prevents a feather from falling as fast as a hammer. On the Moon there is no air, so the feather and hammer fall together.

Page 50
The clock is powered by gravity because the weight (pulled by gravity) keeps the pendulum swinging. Gravity is the only force acting on a pendulum, which makes it

swing back and forth at a constant rate.

Investigate

You will find that the time of swing of a pendulum depends only on its length.

Page 51

1. The Apollo moon walkers could move around easily despite their heavy backpacks, because on the Moon things weigh only one-sixth of what they do on Earth.

2. An object weighing 1,000 newtons on Earth would weigh only about 167 newtons on the Moon, but 2,540 newtons on Jupiter.

Page 52

1. The space shuttle has the power of 37 jumbo jets.

2. The panels are made up of large numbers of solar cells. These devices turn the energy in sunlight into electricity to work the Telescope's instruments and radio transmitters.

Page 53

1. The map of the Earth in 10 million years time will be different from today's map because the Earth's land masses are slowly moving. This is called continental drift.

2. A satellite at a height of 35,900 km (22,300 miles) takes exactly 24 hours to circle the Earth. The Earth also takes 24 hours to spin round once. So if the satellite travels in the direction in which the Earth is spinning, it appears to be fixed in the sky.

Page 54

1. You can't pour yourself a glass of milk because in the weightlessness of space, liquids won't pour. They stay in their container.

2. The pepper would simply float away in the air and be inhaled by all, with general sneezing all round!

3. Astronauts have to 'tie' themselves into their sleeping bags and attach them to something, otherwise they would float away.

Page 55

1. Your muscles start to waste away in zero-g because you are not continually fighting against the pull of gravity. Leg muscles especially are affected, because you cannot walk in zero-g.

2. Nothing happens if you take your finger away, because your colleague is actually suspended in mid-air.

62

Further Reading

Ardley, Neil.
Muscles to Machines.
Aladdin Books, London. 1990.

Catherall, Ed.
Exploring Uses of Energy.
Wayland, Hove. 1990.

Hann, Judith.
Eyewitness Science Guides, How Science Works.
Dorling Kindersley, London. 1991.

Lafferty, Peter.
Eyewitness Science, Force and Motion.
Dorling Kindersley, London. 1992.

Lambert, Andrew.
Physics in Action.
Blackie and Son, London. 1988.

Parker, Steve.
Isaac Newton and Gravity.
Belitha Press, London. 1993.

Science Quest, Forces.
Heinemann, Oxford. 1994.

Taylor, Barbara.
Force and Movement.
Franklin Watts, London. 1990.

Index

(Numbers in italics refer to illustrations)